Africa and The World: Revisited

AKBAR MUHAMMAD

Copyright © 2017 Akbar Muhammad

All rights reserved.

ISBN: 978-1-936937-43-1

First Edition October 2017

Compiled and Edited by Dora Muhammad

Printed by RATHSI Publishing

Atlanta, Georgia

To order additional copies and/or request Akbar Muhammad for speaking engagements contact:

(314) 498-8260/ magnafis@yahoo.com

This book is dedicated to my daughter, Samimah Aziz, who over the years continually encouraged me to put my articles in a book form and complete my autobiography, which God willing, will be my next publication.

ACKNOWLEDGEMENTS

Earl 3X Reddix in Atlanta, Georgia, for his valuable input and invaluable research. Brian E. Muhammad in Columbia, South Carolina, as I could always count on him to critique my articles. Anniyyah Muhammad in Atlanta, Georgia, for typing my original articles into a database and organizing all of my pictures from my many travels. Rashidah Muhammad in Chicago, Illinois, for proofreading the initial collection of my articles selected to appear in this book. Kevin Bryant in St. Louis, Mo., for his tremendous ability as a graphic designer and his wonderful suggestions on how to put information in front of the public. Patrick S. Muhammad at RATHSI Publishing in Atlanta, Georgia, student minister, teacher, principal, publisher and farmer, and a wonderful brother. Dora Muhammad, a beautiful sister and former editor in chief of The Final Call, who stepped to the plate in my time of need to outline and edit the compilation of this book; when I did not think I could get it out in a timely fashion, she made it happen. I am forever grateful to my sister.

CONTENTS

Preface	xiii
Foreword	xv
Part I- Africa In Relationship	6

Section I   7
THE CONTINENT:
AFRICANS AT HOME IN UNITY WITH ONE ANOTHER

Section II   36
THE DIASPORA: A BRIDGE TO AFRICANS ABROAD

Section III   54
AFRICA & THE HONORABLE MINISTER LOUIS FARRAKHAN:
AN INCOMPARABLE BOND

Section IV   68
AFRICA & AKBAR: SENTIMENTS ALONG MY JOURNEY

Section V   83
AFRICA & THE WORLD: GLOBAL AGENDAS

Section VI   103
AFRICA & THE PRESS:
CORRECTING THE DISTORTED LENS OF MULTIMEDIA PROPAGANDA

Part 2- AT THE HEART OF AFRICA

Section VII   137
ECONOMICS & DEVELOPMENT: BUILDING BLOCKS OF FREEDOM

Section VIII   157
WAR & CONFLICT:
THE MORAL ACCOUNTABILITY OF HIDDEN IMPERIALIST HANDS

Section IX   186
POLITICS & GOOD GOVERNANCE:
UNDERSTANDING TRUE MODELS OF LEADERSHIP

Section X   215
LAW & JUSTICE:
THE EFFICACY OF REPARATIONS AND PRISONER RESETTLEMENT

Section XI   249
SOCIAL & CULTURAL CONNECTIONS:
ESSENTIAL SOLUTIONS FOR CHANGE

About the Author	265
Index	267
Article Catalogue	275

PREFACE

I am eternally grateful for the opportunity that I have been afforded to write a column in *The Final Call* newspaper entitled, "Africa and The World." This column appeared in various Black publications in America and Africa. When the *Daily Graphic* newspaper in Ghana printed my article, "My Love of Africa," I was elated. It was on page two of the paper, and I felt that I had an opportunity in my writing to speak to the impact that living in Africa had on me.

And to that end, I thank Minister Louis Farrakhan for assigning me to open the Nation of Islam's first office on the African continent. We called the office, "The Nation of Islam Information Center," and we held discussions and lectures on the Teachings of the Honorable Elijah Muhammad and the direction of Minister Farrakhan as he worked tirelessly to rebuild the work of the Honorable Elijah Muhammad.

As I began to write these articles, I realized that very little knowledge about the struggles on the African continent was being conveyed to Africans in the Diaspora. So, this book, comprised of 68 of my articles, is my contribution to revisit them, and give those who read it an insight to the ongoing struggles of African people on the continent. Many of these articles mention Brother Colonel Muammar Qadhafi. May Allah be pleased with his work, forgive him of his sins, and be pleased with his tremendous love he showed and help given to the Nation of Islam and the movement of Minister Farrakhan throughout the world.

Thank you for purchasing this book. I hope that it in some small way contributes to a greater and better understanding of Africa.

Abdul Akbar Muhammad International Representative of the Honorable Minister Louis Farrakhan and the Nation of Islam.

FOREWORD

When I read the first words of the first chapter of this book, I smiled broadly, as if I had just stepped off an airplane and Brother Abdul Akbar Muhammad was waiting to be my companion on an exotic adventure. And there we were, in Benin.

Akbar Muhammad's perspective on Africa and the world is special. He is an extremely well-read, Muslim scholar and former bookstore owner, who was an assistant first to Minister Malcolm X, and for most of the 51 years since the Honorable Elijah Muhammad sent Minister Louis Farrakhan to Harlem's Muhammad Mosque No. 7, he has been the Minister Farrakhan's faithful companion. Africa-wise, although he hails from the Diaspora, his "African-ness" is beyond question, and it comes through loud and clear in this book.

This well-written series of articles introduces the reader to many of Africa's 54 countries by a guide—no, an ambassador; no, a foreign minister—who hasvisited 44 of Africa's 54 countries since his first visit to Africa in 1976. For 12 years, he was based in Ghana, and has been a frequent visitor to all the hotspots in Africa. Known throughout the African world simply as "Brother Akbar," his intimate familiarity with so, so many of the exotic boat rides, or dirt roads leading from one destination to another once you've reached the Continent is also spiced with horror stories in airports in western capitals. His guidance through the perils of customs inspections is born of experiences where every single scrap of paper in his possession had to be examined on one occasion on his re-entry to the United States.

In addition to the beauty and romance of Africa shared in this book, there are essays explaining, (unraveling, really) African politics, economics, law, culture and even war. He also acquaints us with his remarkable lifelong relationship with Minister Farrakhan.

As a "Welcome to Africa" tour book alone, this would be a great book to check out. But as an encyclopedic study guide for a serious understanding of Africa, its history and politics, this book is an important, required resource. And thank you for the frequent poetic flourishes. Like this: a proverb that Brother Akbar's quotes in "Love of Africa" article: "It is better to see Africa once than to hear about it a thousand times."

"This should be the dream of those in the Diaspora," he writes, "from Casablanca to the Comoros, from Cairo to Cape Town, from Benghazi to Blantyre, from Accra to Addis, from Kumasi to Kisangani, and from Misrata to Mombasa: Africa has soul."

Askia Muhammad

Senior Editor of The Final Call Newspaper

International Representative Abdul Akbar Muhammad
and The Honorable Minister Louis Farrakhan

AFRICA AND THE WORLD: REVISITED

1
My Love Of Africa

In July of this year (1998), I will mark my eighth year of living and traveling in Africa. Duties and circumstances compel me to travel back and forth. It was during a recent trip to Benin that I was able to feel and express in words what my heart has been telling me about the beauty of Africa since I and other Americans do not ever have the opportunity to know. It is definitely unrecognizable, according to the imagery presented by Keith Richburg, a Black American, in his book, "Out of America: A Black Man Confronts Africa." He describes the carnage in Rwanda and Burundi in such a way to turn off anyone who may have positive thoughts about traveling to any part of Africa.

In spite of the negativity of that book, the rhythm of Africa is so profound that you experience it even ona ferry crossing the Gambian River over to Barra in the Gambia. You can see it while driving on the dirt road to Juffureh, the village made famous by Alex Haley, the author of "Roots." This is the real Africa – a place where joy and pain both vie for dominance; and joy wins. It is felt and seen at funerals in Ghana, where the people celebrate the lives of those who have passed on with song and dance.

More rhythms emanate as I ride from Porto-Novo to Cotonou in Benin, crossing the swamps and look out at the dugout boats and see the beautiful ebony bodies in the fishermen striking their oars in the water. This is a natural fitness center and part of their daily routine to eke out a living. The unique postures of the Black women who walk with such grace were developed from years of balancing their wares on their heads. Africa without fabrics of colorful prints and colorful bubbas would not be Africa at all.

AKBAR MUHAMMAD

I love the Nigerians for maintaining a national dress. Ghana also has a national dress for women, which is called a *kaba*. I can feel pain for those lands and countries where the colonial masters robbed the people of a national dress and put them in "brand name lookalike" jeans, T-shirts and tennis shoes. The pain can be eased, however, with their proper connection to their culture.

Africa, your sons and daughters in the Diaspora will love you oh so much more once they get to know you. You can only take away from Africa what you bring to its shores. If you bring the colonial mind of arrogance with the attitude of 'I am better than you because I come from America, Europe, Canada or the Caribbean,' don't expect Africa to give you anything since you see Africa through the minds and eyes of your former masters.

There is an African proverb that confirms this idea: "It is better to see Africa once than to hear about it a thousand times." This should be the dream of those in the Diaspora – from Casablanca to the Comoros, from Cairo to Cape Town, from Benghazi to Blantyre, from Accra to Addis, from Kumasi to Kisangani, and from Misrata to Mombasa; Africa has soul.

Only those who know Africa can understand why a consummate struggler for African liberation such as Brother Kwame Ture – who was born in the Caribbean (Trinidad), raised in America and moved to Africa by the time he was 30 – would want to go home to Africa in the sunset of his life. *It is his love of Africa.*

2
AIRPORT BLUES FOR THE AFRICAN IN EUROPE

The airport in Rome is about the worst I have experienced.

It starts when any flight from an African destination lands at Fiumicino Airport. First, you are taken through a special door for health and sanitation and given a yellow card warning you that you may have been exposed to diseases in the country from which you are traveling. This is a total insult!

After you receive the card, you then proceed to a line where an arrogant Italian immigration officer examines your passport. In a tone of indignation, he questions your reason for coming there, while he holds your passport up to the light to see if your picture has been replaced. He examines your visa closely and checks the other visas in your passport and asks what kind of business you're in. He then begins to interrogate you as if you are a criminal. His other hand waves through passengers with white skin, without checking their passports. They could be smugglers, they could have forged documents or they could be criminals. However, the color of their skin gives them a clearance badge at most European airports.

AKBAR MUHAMMAD

Upon clearance through this line, you then proceed to another line and endure the same type of harassment again before your bags go through a scanning machine. In many cases, the officers hold up your passport, then act as if they have some suspicion of you and tell you to stand aside for no apparent reason. Then, they go into a nearby office to "check you out" and the line is held up even longer.

On one of my recent trips, I was incensed by the way they were handling the Ghanaian and Nigerian brothers and sisters. When my turn came to hand an officer my passport, he began to examine my credentials as if they were just printed. I asked him, "What is the problem?" He did not look up at me nor did he answer me. At the same time, he waved through some more Europeans without examining their passports.

I questioned him loud enough for the African brothers and sisters to hear, "Is this some kind of racist policy where Black people are questioned like they are criminals and Europeans can just pass through?" He responded, "We examine Americans also and just because you are an American, don't think that you are different from anyone else." I quickly responded, "That was not my question nor did I ask you that."

He was trying to infer to the rest of the Africans that, because I had an American passport, I did not want to be questioned in the manner in which he was questioning them. I became very loud, however I maintained my composure and repeated, "That's not what I'm talking about here. I am talking about you passing White people through while you harass Black people. The White people are not stopped, but the African people are."

This went on for a few minutes. All of the African brothers were looking at me and some looked a little embarrassed. However, I wanted to encourage them to have the strength to stand up and not allow themselves to go through this harassment. When you go through Amsterdam, you have the same problem. Many of the Africans are just so happy to get a visa that they will tolerate unfair treatment.

AFRICA AND THE WORLD: REVISITED

In Amsterdam after deplaning, an announcement is made that, if your plane has come from an African country, to "have your passports ready." The painful experience is that you get in a line and wait as they examine passports, visas and tickets, and question you, while White people are able to pass quickly through. Many White passengers hold up their passports just so the cover shows and are waved right through without harassment, while Black people are being visibly harassed like common criminals.

I call it the "African Blues at European Airports." This ill treatment however reflects the growing trend and mood in Europe to rid itself of Africans and others from so-called Third World nations. When Europeans come to African nations, they are treated very well. Sometimes while waiting in line, they are beckoned to come to the front by Africans standing in line or officials who bring them through the quick service, trying to give them traditional African hospitality.

AKBAR MUHAMMAD

AFRICA
IN RELATIONSHIP

AFRICA AND THE WORLD: REVISITED
THE CONTINENT: AFRICANS AT HOME IN UNITY WITH ONE ANOTHER

Akbar Muhammad, Minister Louis Farrakhan, Mummar Quadaffi

Minister Louis Farrakhan, Alpha Omar Konare former Pres. of Mali, Akbar Muhammad, Sam Nujoma- Pres. of Namibia, Mutar Ganass, Daniel Ortega Pres of Nicaragua in Namibia

AKBAR MUHAMMAD

Minister Louis Farrakhan delivering message on Muhammad Ali Day in Kingston, Jamaica during his first visit to the island, which was organized by Akbar Muhammad (pictured, bottom left) (1975)

3

Colonel Muammar Qadhafi Speaks on Reparations to Black Americans for Slavery and a United States of Africa

At the invitation of Muammar Qadhafi, an African American press delegation was granted an exclusive interview with the Libyan leader on the heels of the very successful Organization of African Unity (OAU) Extraordinary Meeting in Sirte, Libya. The delegation was led by Akbar Muhammad and included freelance writer Jehron Hunter of Philadelphia, Pennsylvania, writing for African American newspapers in the Delaware Valley; photojournalist Monica Morgan of Detroit, Michigan and James Muhammad, Editor-in-Chief of *The Final Call* newspaper in Chicago, Illinois.

Qadhafi's passion to work on the unification of Africa was consistently expressed throughout the interview. After seven years of sanctions and embargoes, he appeared energized and ready to move his country forward. His vision for a United States of Africa and the trial of two Libyan nationals, which is scheduled to start in February 2000, seem to be on the top of his agenda. He claimed that the two accused are innocent and they will be cleared of all charges. He is also author of "The Green Book," his thoughts on a new social world order, published in 1977.

AKBAR MUHAMMAD

During the interview, through an interpreter, Qadhafi articulated his strong desire to see Africans in the Diaspora involved in the process of forming a United States of Africa. He invited Africans in the Diaspora to join a conference of non-governmental organizations (NGOs) of Africa. The conference will take place the first week of February 2000. At this conference, he will discuss how Africans in the Diaspora and NGOs can move the process for the United States of Africa forward.

African American Press Delegation (AAPD): *When you first launched the revolution, you had a particular thought and goal in mind. What was your desire for Libya then and how has it evolved over the last 30 years?*

Muammar Qadhafi (MQ): The objective was to liberate Libya because Libya was a colonized country. At that time, it had five American military bases, a few British military bases and 20,000 Italian settlers. They controlled all the economic activity and all the arable land. The revolution I had in mind was to change Libya. We feel that we have put forward and submitted a theory that may change the world. Even though the current generation may not understand and fully grasp this theory, the forthcoming generation will be able to grasp it and understand it fully.

AAPD: *How relevant is "The Green Book" today in light of the changes that have taken place in the world?*

MQ: Whatever is taking place in developments and changes in the world is an explanation and interpretation of "The Green Book." An example is that, when nobody thought there would be a separation in the Soviet Union or Czechoslovakia or Yugoslavia, "The Green Book" prophesied and stated that countries that have many nationalities one day would break up into smaller nationalist entities. Such a thing happened. The Soviet Union was broken up according to the nationalist entities. Yugoslavia was broken up.

AFRICA AND THE WORLD: REVISITED

Such a thing may also apply to the United States of America because, if the United States of America is composed of various races, nationalities and nationalist entities, then one day there will be a conflict and they will break up and form their own nationalist entities. Even India, if it is composed of various religions and nationalities, one day will break up and they will separate from each other. Also in "The Green Book," it is stated that the workers, the wage earners, one day will become partners despite the will of the owners, the employers. Today, we have seen so many big companies giving property and shares to the wage earners. This popular socialism, which is heralded by "The Green Book," is being imposed on the world now.

AAPD: *In an interview that you gave to the Inside The Middle East magazine in 1983, a question was asked about mistakes that have been made, and you were quoted as saying there were mistakes made in good faith. Can you talk about some of the alleged mistakes that they suggested that you made in the formulation of the Jamahiriya?*

MQ: For sure there may have been some mistakes because we learn from life and experiences. When you work, you are bound to make mistakes. Also, the changes that took place in the world also should be taken into consideration.

AAPD: *In 1982, the 19th Assembly of the OAU was scheduled to take place here in Tripoli. However, that meeting did not take place because a quorum wasn't reached and the meeting was cancelled. It was said that 19 states boycotted the meeting. What do you think was the real reason that they did not show up?*

MQ: At the time, they were traitorous governments and America was able to give them orders not to go to Tripoli. There were one or two countries less than the needed two-thirds quorum.

AAPD: *Then in 1999, some 43 heads of state came here for a special session of the OAU. What made the difference?*

MQ: It is because the stooges have been taken off the throne. America actually loses when it depends on traitorous or stooge governments and when it depends on agents and traitors. America should acknowledge the will of the African people. The will of the African people will be victorious in the end. If America wants to have a mutual interest with Africa, she should then respect Africa. The policy of creating stooges and traitors and the policy of replacing patriotic and nationalist governments is a policy that is doomed to fail.

First of all, people will hate America because of this policy. The second reason is that the stooges or traitors made by America will not live forever. They cannot continue. One day, they will be overthrown. The change, in this case, will be against America because the governments or systems that have been changed are traitorous. These leaders were made by America. The people will overthrow them and, thus, the people will hate America for supporting such leaders. This is a piece of advice from me to America.

AAPD: *When the United States of Africa becomes a reality, what kind of leader will it take to run it? Will you be a candidate?*

MQ: Excuse me, but don't put this question in this way. Allow me to say that, because we don't want to focus on who will be in government or who will rule. This will cause us to deviate from the noble objective and great work to a lower level. We want Africa to be united and we want Africa to govern itself by itself. We don't want anyone to rule Africa.

AAPD: *The West continues to use the terminology "sub-Saharan Africa" and "North Africa" instead of "Africa" as a whole. Do you think this is intentional?*

AFRICA AND THE WORLD: REVISITED

MQ: This is a malicious policy but it is exposed. They want to define Africa geographically and from the ethnic point of view. But Africans themselves have made the Sahara Desert a bridge, not a partition. The proof of that is now there are more than one million African Blacks coming to Libya to work from those countries that are supposed to be sub-Saharan. The desert did not prevent them from coming to Libya.

AAPD: *U.S. Secretary of State Madeleine Albright just finished a visit to Africa, visiting six countries. Some would say there is a new initiative to gain influence in Africa by America and France. How do you view her trip in light of your work to unite Africa?*

MQ: It seems that France is tired of Africa. It is slowing down and deserting Africa. And the same thing will happen to America. Africa will present a burden to anyone who covets Africa. In the future, Africa will become awakened and the Western powers will not get anything out of Africa because she will be awakened. Both ways, the Western powers are losers.

AAPD: *In America, the conflict in the Sudan that you have been working to resolve is portrayed as Muslims fighting against Christians who want to be free of an Islamic government. The Southern leader, John Garang is being supported by America through surrogate countries such as Uganda, Kenya, Ethiopia and Eritrea. How do you see this conflict being resolved? Will America withdraw the aid from John Garang and force him to a peace table, or will they continue to aid him and let this conflict go on?*

MQ: This is one of the failed American policies. John Garang will never be an agent of America. Recently, he spoke to me on the telephone and told me that, even though he was in America, he is still a revolutionary; and whether or not he goes to America will not affect his revolutionary spirit. It will not change him. Both ways, America will be a loser. If America wants to fight the world, it will lose. If America wants to involve itself in the affairs of the world to give assistance to the world and be involved all over the world, it will get tired, depleted and sap itself; and in the end, it will lose.

AAPD: *Then how can the civil war be resolved?*

MQ: Personally speaking, I see no good reason that makes the Sudanese fight each other. It is an internal problem to start with. But bear in mind that, with the mentality that is prevalent now, the problem may not be solved. If we look thoroughly and deeply into the problem, we don't find a very real or serious reason for the war. The problem is the mentality or the way of thinking of the people there. Once there is a change in the mentality and way of thinking in the people in the Sudan, there won't be a problem.

In the meantime, I won't give any reasons to oblige the Southerners to fight me. If I were Garang, I could not find any reason, justification or necessity for young people to die and suffer all the hardships to make them go to war to fight. It is possible, politically speaking, that dialogue can be engaged. I regret it and it bothers me to say that the war has changed into a matter of business.

AAPD: *You talked about reparations in your recent messages to African heads of state. Do you feel that the American government should pay reparations to the descendants of slaves and what do you think would be fair compensation?*

AFRICA AND THE WORLD: REVISITED

MQ: This is an obligation of America and one day America will be obliged and forced to pay the price. America is suffering from megalomania, and her ears and eyes are shut because of her power and strength. But one day, America's might will come to an end and America will open her eyes and ears to see and hear the truth. Compensation should be both moral and material.

AAPD: *In the United States of Africa, what role do you see Africans in the Diaspora playing?*

MQ: They have a role to play. The work and the call for African unity actually started from Africans who work outside of Africa. It dates back to the 1900s and it started from the Manchester conference in England. Africans in the Diaspora at the time started covering themselves and holding conferences to talk about liberating their own land and uniting.

Judging by that, Africans who are in the Diaspora have a big role to play. They should help their people who are inside the Motherland. They should mobilize them and raise their morale. The Jews do that similarly all over the world. They encouraged the creation of the state of Israel and they give the state of Israel money and moral support. Even though they are Americans, they work to actually make America give service to Israel. They do not forget their ancestors. They do not forget that they are Jews. By the same token, this applies to the Black Africans in America. Even if they become rulers and presidents one day, they should not forget their mother, Africa.

AAPD: *We have in America 1.8 million prisoners in jail and most of them are Black, Hispanic and Native American. Brother Minister Louis Farrakhan in his book, "Torchlight for America," talks about having a program that will bring prisoners who have been reformed to Africa to help in the development of Africa. What do you think of that idea?*

MQ: That is a very good idea and we welcome it. Africa should do that because they are the sons of Africa. That's their mother. Africa is their home.

AAPD: *What role did Nelson Mandela and Prince Bandar bin Sultan of Saudi Arabia play in your decision to release the two Libyan nationals accused of the Pan Am bombing over Lockerbie to a third country for trial? Also, what would be your message to the family members of the Pan Am victims?*

MQ: It goes without saying that the Lockerbie issue is a tragedy. The relatives of the victims need consolation. But all of us should know the truth of who did that and we should know the reason behind it. It seems that the action was not done by a lunatic. According to the information, evidence and theories that have now been provided by the authorities, it seems that the action was carefully planned and very well executed, to the extent that I don't believe that Third World countries could actually perform it. Because it was so highly pieced together and so well-planned, some believe it was actually the work of American Intelligence. I mean it was pre-planned.

But what is the cause? Is it to take revenge on the American government? Is it an action against the policy of America because it has taken an action against a people? Or is it because America herself knows that there are certain quarters or certain organizations in the world that want revenge against America? So American Intelligence may actually plan such an action so that the direction of these parties will be diverted and people will think these parties have taken revenge against America. The American Intelligence will do such an action so that others will accuse those certain quarters because they have a grudge against America.

AFRICA AND THE WORLD: REVISITED

For instance, if America wants to take any action against Libya, then America will direct its Intelligence to do a piece of work to the extent that it will claim that Libya had done it, if Libya was able and capable to do it. Since Libya is not able to do such an action (Lockerbie), American Intelligence fulfilled this action and Libya is accused. Then, the American government will find justification for action to be taken against Libya. This seems to be the case as far as Lockerbie is concerned.

In 1986, America killed Libyan women and children and destroyed houses of the Libyan people, so the families of the children wish to take revenge against America. And because Libyans cannot actually do it, American Intelligence does it and Libya is incriminated. America then has justification to impose sanctions against Libya. It seems that this is the scenario.

AAPD: It is said in some papers that Libya lost $20-$30 billion during the seven years of sanctions. If the suspects are found innocent, will Libya sue America and the Western world for the money and lives they lost during these sanctions?

MQ: Of course, if such a thing happens, then we shall go to the Security Council of the United Nations and we shall ask for reparations and compensation because we have paid the price for an action that we did not commit. For this reason, America wants to condemn Libya and convict Libya one way or the other. We know that America is working to influence the Scottish judiciary and wants to create false eyewitnesses. America actually pays money to create unreal witnesses. We even know the names of a few witnesses who are false because they are being paid by America. One of them is named Abdul Majeed Jaaka. He's Libyan. The judges and the court will be bothered by American influence and pressures.

AKBAR MUHAMMAD

AAPD: *What is your message to young people in America? Also, what music do you like to listen to?*

MQ: I like classical music. I like Beethoven. My message to young people is that I wish a new generation will be created in America, a new generation that will put an end to the imperialist and reactionary America. That this new generation will enable and empower the American people to govern themselves by themselves. That they will continue to protest this false democracy and, perhaps in the future, they will boycott the elections. I would hope that the youth will exploit and utilize the potential and resources of America for the betterment of humanity, not to the detriment of mankind as it is taking place today.

AAPD: *At the Islamic World Peoples Leadership Conference in 1995 in Benghazi, you said that Libya and the Islamic world should put $1 billion in place for Minister Farrakhan, leader of the Nation of Islam, to use in rebuilding the African American communities in America. What is your thinking on that at this time?*

MQ: My thinking is the same.

AAPD: *In America, we have an unbalanced view of Muammar Qadhafi. Can you tell us who is the Qadhafi that the West does not know?*

MQ: Qadhafi is different and contrary to what America says now and what Americans know about him. Anything that American media says is different from the true Qadhafi.

AAPD: *Thank you.*

4

RE-EXAMINING MUAMMAR QADHAFI'S CALL FOR A UNITED STATES OF AFRICA

The call is not new. However, Pan-Africanists worldwide were glad to hear it again. In September 1998, Muammar Qadhafi, leader of the Libyan Revolution, made several announcements that the world press muted. In February of this year, the Libyan press repeated and revisited many of those same announcements.

During my recent visit to Libya, the Libyan people were celebrating the one year anniversary of establishing unity with the African states of Mali, Chad, Niger, Burkina Faso and the Sudan. The celebration was centered on Libya's working alliance with the leaders of these African states. The Libyan people celebrated the leaders for showing strength in the face of the UN (United Nations) embargo to fly their planes to Tripoli. Other Africans shared with the Libyan people the belief that the sanctions and embargoes against Libya, backed by the United States and the United Kingdom, are unjust.

The countries represented by African leaders who dared to defy the unjust sanctions and flew directly to Tripoli are Djibouti, the Sudan, Chad, Niger, Burkina Faso, Mali, the Gambia, Malawi, Central African Republic, Democratic Republic of Congo (formerly Zaire), Namibia and Eritrea.

AKBAR MUHAMMAD

The negotiations over the two Libyan nationals accused for the Pan Am 103 bombing over Lockerbie, Scotland are now ending. There is confusion as to why Muammar Qadhafi did not immediately turn over his nationals to the world court in the Netherlands. Qadhafi described the agreement between the United Kingdom (UK), America and the Netherlands as "an act of piracy." Instead of remaining in the Netherlands to stand trial, they would have been transferred to the UK.

This point was clear with the capture of the Kurdish leader, Abdullah Ocalan in Kenya. The deception took place with the aid of the CIA and the Israeli Intelligence. Ocalan attempted to take refuge in one country and was turned over to another. Qadhafi kept saying that there was an inroad for an act of piracy in the proposal submitted by America and the UK, which needed clarification and preventive measures put in place.

During the past year, Qadhafi has focused Libya's attention southward to become more involved in affairs of the African continent, despite attempts to isolate Libya by the West. Some of the points made by Qadhafi at his call to redirect Libya's focus on Africa include:

> 1. He pronounced that Libyan television, which for years had shown a map of the Arab world, now shows the map of Africa. In October 1998, Libya started its "Voice of Africa" radio program that broadcasts in Arabic, English and French. It broadcasts on both shortwave and medium-wavebands and reaches most African nations. The future plans are for the program to be broadcast in Fulani, Hausa and Swahili.

> 2. He called for the wise men of Africa to come together and look at how they can strike down the lines of demarcation on the African continent.

> 3. He called for a United States of Africa, saying, "There should be no divisions on the African continent, from Pretoria to Tripoli." He also said that he wished to make Libya a nucleus for African unity.

4. He said that Africa has the potential to be a paradise for its people and hell for its enemies.

5. He said that Africa is for the Africans, and those who cannot accept and have a problem with the Black color of most Africans should leave, further stating that they should cross the sea and find somewhere else to live.

6. If the United Nations (UN) is really a democratic body, then the power of the Security Council should shift to the General Assembly, which includes all nations. It is a body that should be the decision maker – the body that holds the first and the last. The Security Council should be the arm that implements decisions of the General Assembly. He added that what is taking place at the UN is a falsification of international law.

7. Concerning Libyan women, he said, "There are African women who are intimately involved in the Jamahiriya People's Authority." The women have at their disposal the resources of Jamahiriya, its weapons and education. He described them as free and happy in the Jamahiriya culture. He said that they could be an example for women who are truly free around the world.

8. Finally, he thanked all the African leaders involved in the decision in Ouagadougou, Burkina Faso last year to disregard the unjust sanctions led by the United States of America and United Kingdom against his country. He thanked all African leaders for showing true African revolutionary spirit and the capability to shoulder their historical responsibility as Africans. They will not let outsiders isolate one of the brotherly states with sanctions or blockades. He said, "We are marching towards a United States of Africa."

AKBAR MUHAMMAD

In a savage world that is dominated by the West, a United States of Africa is not a luxury, but a necessity. The real issue that Africa faces today is "to be or not to be." All indications show that Africans insist on the first option.

5

Will The African Union Be Delayed By September 11

Those who have followed the news from the continent may have noticed that there has been very little discussion about the African Union since September 11 and America's ongoing war against terrorism and nations that have been historically classified by America and some of her allies as rogue nations and its leaders classified as pariahs.

The nation that has been pushing the process of the African Union falls into this category. This is the country of Libya. Because of the tragedy of September 11, those who have been applauding and supporting the effort of Libyan leader Muammar Qadhafi toward the African Union have noticed the silence on this issue. Africans in the Diaspora, in particular, applauded this effort, for we saw it as a vehicle for dual citizenship and for Africans to have one united Africa.

Again, those who take a keen interest in Africa felt that the African Union would be the vehicle that would solve many of the political crises that Africa is facing at the present time. The problems in Liberia are now again on the front page. Here is a tragedy of tremendous proportion.

The Liberian people have thought at last that they can return home and have some semblance of normalcy in their lives, only to see the population fleeing out of the capital and death in the countryside, while the government of President Charles Taylor struggles to maintain order and power as the legitimate representative of the Liberian people.

The tragedy of Liberia is only a sign of what could happen all across Africa. The continuous meetings that were held to discuss the African Union allowed leaders of Africa to come together and see each other. Side meetings were used to discuss some of the differences and problems facing their countries. Without these meetings, we can see that Africa is falling into the miserable state of war and conflict that it faced before the emergence of the Sirte Declaration 9/9/99.

We would hope that Africans at home and abroad should hope for the continuation of this process. We do not want to see July 2002 in Pretoria become a meeting that goes nowhere, realizing that we are facing the challenge that an African who is an Arab has led the call for a United States of Africa.

6

United States Of Africa –

The End Of The Organization Of African Unity And The Birth Of The African Union

At the invitation of Muammar Qadhafi, leader of the Libyan Revolution, Minister Louis Farrakhan and his delegation attended the 37th Organization of African Unity (OAU) Conference held in Lusaka, Zambia July 9-12, 2001. More than 35 heads of state from the African continent were represented at the conference. Since the celebration of the 30th anniversary of the OAU in Cairo, Egypt in July 1994, this conference was the next most historical gathering because it marked the end of the OAU and the beginning of the African Union.

Minister Farrakhan and his delegation were the only representatives of Africans in the Diaspora. In a private meeting before he delivered his speech, Muammar Qadhafi told Minister Farrakhan that the idea of a united Africa came from Africans in the Diaspora. He said, "This is why it is important for Africans in the Diaspora to not only support this initiative but also be a part of this process."

AKBAR MUHAMMAD

Later when Qadhafi was called to the podium to deliver a closing address to the heads of state, he asked the conference chairman to allow Minister Farrakhan to have a few words. Minister Farrakhan stressed, in public, what he had said in private, that Africans in the Diaspora are important to the process.

Qadhafi made a strong appeal to the conference coordinators to permit Minister Farrakhan, a leader of Africans in the Diaspora, to further address the conference. In the middle of his appeal, there was a power failure and the auditorium went black. Brother Qadhafi's security surrounded him while waiting for the lighting to be restored. Supreme Captain Mustapha Farrakhan and Sultan Muhammad immediately surrounded Minister Farrakhan. When the power was restored, Brother Qadhafi concluded his remarks.

Conference host Frederick Chiluba, President of Zambia who takes his term for one year as the head of the newly formed African Union, did not acknowledge the request of Brother Qadhafi and he proceeded to offer his closing remarks. The talk in the conference was that the blackout was intentional; however, it was blamed on a mysterious fire at the power station. The next day, one of the newspapers said the power was intentionally cut and the fire was an act of sabotage.

This trip was a long and difficult one, and took Minister Farrakhan from Chicago to Zurich, Switzerland, and then to Johannesburg, South Africa, nonstop. Then, he traveled in a private plane for more than 24 hours from Johannesburg to Lusaka, Zambia. Minister Farrakhan met with many heads of state after the conference to discuss pressing problems and challenges of the various countries and regions of Africa.

AFRICA AND THE WORLD: REVISITED

He had an extensive conversation with Robert Mugabe, President of Zimbabwe, on the issue of land being returned to its original owners – the Black people of Zimbabwe. With President Joaquim Chissano of Mozambique, he discussed the state of the economy and the aftermath of the tremendous floods that have devastated the country. He talked to President Yoweri Museveni of Uganda and, as a result, he was invited to return to Uganda. He spoke with President Ahmad Tejan Kabbah of Sierra Leone about the current struggle to stabilize the government. He held extensive talks with Omar al-Bashir, President of the Sudan, concerning the attack on his government regarding the question of slavery. He also met with the new presidents of Ghana, Somalia and Cote D'Ivoire and exchanged greetings with President Olusegun Obasanjo of Nigeria, President Thabo Mbeki of South Africa and President Sam Nujoma of Namibia.

AKBAR MUHAMMAD

7

Farrakhan Calls For Support For African Union

Having just returned from the July 9-11 Organization of African Unity (OAU) Summit in Lusaka, Zambia that birthed the African Union (AU), the Honorable Minister Louis Farrakhan said it is important that Blacks in the Diaspora unite behind the efforts put forth by the African heads of state. The Summit was the 37th and final meeting of the OAU, and was attended by 41 heads of state. Now it will be known as the African Union, a constitutional body that will establish such institutions as a Central Bank and common African currency, a Parliament, Court of Justice, a national defense force, and other continental institutions. Planners hope that the African Union eventually will evolve into a United States of Africa.

"I personally felt blessed to witness both a sunset and a sunrise," Minister Farrakhan said in a congratulatory letter printed in the July 24th edition of *The Final Call*. "The setting sun gives us pause to reflect on the activity of the day, the mistakes, errors and accomplishments that we might make the next day better.

"Sunrise offers us the hope that the new day will be better than the past day if we learned the lessons of yesterday. The sunset of the OAU, after 38 years, gives Africa much to reflect on its successes and failures; and the sunrise of the African Union gives us much hope if we are able to learn from the mistakes of the past," he said.

AKBAR MUHAMMAD

Minister Farrakhan said much had to be overcome for the heads of state and government to get to the point of establishing the AU, indicating that the Western media ignored the historic event. Powerful governments that the media represent do not want to see the success of a united Africa. He commended African governments for recognizing that "Africa cannot survive in the present era of globalization if she remains as she was, a loosely united group of nations in a loosely united Organization of African Unity.

"Africa can only survive if the present leaders recognize that it is better to be the tail of something than the head of nothing. A United Africa would ensure that all of the sons and daughters of Africa on the African continent could be educated, cultivated and developed to bring about not only a renaissance in Africa, but throughout the world," he said.

Minister Farrakhan, in three World Friendship Tours to the African continent in the last five years, issued a call for the establishment of a United States of Africa on each occasion. In the letter, he also commended Libyan Leader Colonel Muammar Qadhafi, who has spearheaded the recent movement for the African Union. This effort was first launched at the insistence of Africans in the Diaspora. The idea was later pushed in Africa by such great leaders as Kwame Nkrumah of Ghana, Sekou Ture of Guinea and Gamal Abdel Nasser of Egypt.

"African leaders have a great responsibility," Minister Farrakhan warned. "Though many of these leaders are former military men who fought in the liberation struggle for their people, now each of these leaders must become a teacher of profound magnitude in order for the African Union to become a reality.

"We hope to inform all of those in the West who love Africa of the tremendous need for us in the West to form a united front to encourage the bold step that these leaders have taken. We must discourage the political intervention of enemies and their deceitful ideas that are designed to destroy the birth of the infant African Union," Minister Farrakhan said.

AFRICA AND THE WORLD: REVISITED

[The following text is an open letter written by Minister Louis Farrakhan upon his return from the July 9-11 Organization of African Unity (OAU) Summit in Lusaka, Zambia, congratulating African leaders on the establishment of an African Union. Minister Farrakhan was the only leader from the African Diaspora to attend the Summit sessions. The African Union is the new continental structure that will establish a Central Bank and common African currency, an African Parliament and a Court of Justice, among other institutions.]

The Birth of the African Union By the Honorable Minister Louis Farrakhan

In The Name of Allah, The Beneficent, The Merciful

I, my son and Supreme Captain Mustapha Farrakhan, Akbar Muhammad, Sultan Muhammad, and my daughter and nurse Fatima Farrakhan Muhammad were among those who were blessed to be present at the end of the 38 years of the Organization of African Unity (OAU) and witness the beginning or the birth of the African Union toward the ultimate United States of Africa. Many great things have come to birth from very humble beginnings. The most notable was Jesus the Christ, who came to birth in a lowly ox stall or manger. Likewise, the African Union came to birth in a very humble place in Africa, the beautiful country of Zambia, under the leadership of President Frederick Chiluba. Zambia is a country suffering from immense poverty, unemployment, health issues, economic, political and social turbulence. Yet, in this humble and beautiful country, the African Union was born.

AKBAR MUHAMMAD

I personally felt blessed to witness both a sunset and a sunrise. The setting sun gives us pause to reflect on the activity of the day; the mistakes, errors and accomplishments, that we might make the next day better. Sunrise offers us the hope that the new day will be better than the past day if we learned the lesson of yesterday. The sunset of the OAU, after 38 years, gives Africa much to reflect on its successes and failures; and the sunrise of the African Union gives us much hope if we are able to learn from the mistakes of the past in order that we might make a bright future for Africa.

Human beings have been coming to birth on this earth for untold billions and even trillions of years. Yet, of the many billions of human beings who have occupied this earth, history has recorded only a few. In the history of the last 6,000 years, only those who have done the very best and the very worst have had their names etched in history that we might study their lives, successes and failures. Very few human beings have embraced immortality. We come to birth, we live, we die, and we lie forgotten in the sands of time. But I saw 41 heads of state who were present and other heads of state who were absent who had a chance to touch immortality by becoming the Founding Fathers of a New Africa where the whole Continent can become one Great Nation, a Super Power in the 21st century.

Much had to be overcome for these heads of state and government to reach this level of maturity to be able to see the bigger picture, which is that Africa cannot survive in the present era of globalization if she remains as she was, a loosely united group of nations in a loosely united Organization of African Unity. Africa can only survive if the present leaders recognize that it is better to be the tail of something than the head of nothing. A United Africa would ensure that all of the sons and daughters of Africa on the African Continent could be educated, cultivated and developed to bring about not only a renaissance in Africa, but throughout the world. This forming of an African Union, spearheaded by Libyan leader Muammar Qadhafi, was a great and marvelous step in the right direction – a step applauded by all of the sons and daughters of Africa in the Western hemisphere who have been made aware of this new and wonderful, potentially powerful and magnificent development.

The Western media, so upset at the thought of an African Union, has not seen fit to make it newsworthy to the nearly 200 million sons and daughters of Africa living in the Western hemisphere. This teaches us that the owners of the Western media and the powerful governments they represent do not desire to see the success of the African Union. This is a time of great danger for the idea of African Unity. Although it is an idea whose time has come, it can be no stronger than the will and determination of the African leaders to make it a reality. The best time to destroy any idea, plan or organization is in its infancy. So, *the African Union is now in the time of its greatest danger*. The Wester Powers are sifting the African leaders to find those who still have selfish and vain ideas in their hearts and minds that they might be pulled away from the idea of the African Union.

Jesus said to Peter, "The devil desires you that he may sift you as wheat." The Western Powers are sifting the African leaders for character flaws and weaknesses that might be exploited to weaken the idea, the effectiveness and even break the will of those whose desire is to make the African Union a success. Muammar Qadhafi, the Great Leader of the Al-Fatah Revolution and the man who is responsible for pioneering the efforts of the African Union, invited me and members of the Nation of Islam to witness this historic event.

In my Friendship Tour of Africa several years ago, in every African State that I visited, I spoke of and encouraged Africans to think of a United States of Africa. In a private meeting with Muammar Qadhafi in Zambia, he said to me, "*The idea of African unity did not start in Africa. It started in America from the Blacks of the Western Hemisphere, mainly the Caribbean and the United States.*" He said that, "*Since the idea started from the Blacks, the sons and daughters of Africa in the Western Hemisphere, this African Union must be fostered by Blacks in the Diaspora, and the leaders of Africa must be encouraged and even morally pressured that they may understand that they are on a right course and that they must stay this course until it is successfully established.*"

To this end, Libyan Leader Muammar Qadhafi encouraged the Host, President Frederick Chiluba and others to allow Louis Farrakhan to speak and represent the Blacks of the Western Hemisphere. Unfortunately, that request was not honored.

Some 36 years ago, Malcolm X had prepared a speech to address the OAU. There were some African leaders who desired him to speak but there were others who feared that he might say something that would anger the Western Powers and damage their credibility, particularly with England, France and America. Unfortunately, that same fear exists today.

The African leaders have a great responsibility. Though many of these leaders are former military men who fought in the liberation struggle for their people, now each of these leaders must become a teacher of profound magnitude in order for the African Union to become a reality. Each leader and teacher must recognize that their frail political reality is based upon a tribal, ethnic, religious and racial reality that can become very unstable.

If these tribal, ethnic, religious and racial realities in the Nations of Africa become unstable and these divisions are exploited by outside forces, it can have the effect of an earthquake which topples powerful buildings. Likewise, these frail political realities can come tumbling down. There is an answer and solution to these problems of ethnic, tribal, religious and racial differences that are found in the scriptures in both Bible and Qur'an. If the leaders are unaware of these solutions and/or ignorant of how to utilize these solutions that have already been given to these problems, then the African Union and its success is as far away from us as we are far away from understanding the solutions to these problems that are already given in the Wise Revelations of Allah (God) through the mouths of His Prophets.

AFRICA AND THE WORLD: REVISITED

We hope to inform all of those in the West who love Africa of the need for us in the West to form a united front to encourage the bold step that these leaders have taken; and to discourage the political intervention of enemies and their deceitful ideas that are designed to destroy the birth of the infant African Union. No matter what we, as Black people, accomplish in the many countries of the Western Hemisphere in which we live, if Africa is weak, divided, underdeveloped and unhealthy, then our accomplishments are minimized. But, if Africa becomes strong, healthy, united, developed and powerful, no matter where the sons and daughters of Africa are anywhere on this earth, we too will bask in the light of Africa's successful development.

There are many Chinese in the Western Hemisphere who are not communist, but the revolution that brought Mao Tse Tung into power made China a world power. Every Chinese person on this earth, whether communist or not, wears their Chinese heritage with pride. This same pride and joy will come to every son and daughter of Africa when our beloved Africa is united, free and fully developed.

May Allah (God) bless the leaders of the African continent. May He bless Brother Muammar Qadhafi that he will not be discouraged in pursuing the idea of the United States of Africa to its ultimate conclusion. And may Allah (God) bless the sons and daughters of Africa to form a united front wherever we are found, to encourage the African Union to ultimately become the United States of Africa.

Thank you for reading these few words.

AKBAR MUHAMMAD

II
THE DIASPORA:
A BRIDGE TO AFRICANS ABROAD

Akbar Muhammad (r) at the W.E.B. Du Bois Centre in Accra, Ghana, joined by (l-r) Maya Angelou, Kwame Ture and Dr. Ruth Love (1990s)

8

W.E.B. DuBois Submitting To The Call Of Africa

February 23, 1997 will mark the 129th birthday of Dr. W.E.B. Du Bois. Recently, while I was in Cairo, his son Dr. David Du Bois talked about his father's life. He showed me the letter his father wrote that was not to be opened until after his death. Since the Nation of Islam's Saviours' Day Celebration keynote address to the public by Minister Louis Farrakhan this year will also be on February 23rd, I thought I would cover in "Africa and The World" a very small part of a larger-than-life man who was steeped in controversy but never lost focus on his mission as a social intellectual activist.

Dr. W.E.B. Du Bois fought with his pen, mind and body against forces of oppression until his last day - August 27, 1963 – one day before the August 28, 1963 March on Washington, D.C. When we read certain aspects about his full life, we cannot help but think about the battles with the government of America regarding his international travel. The government of America took his passport on two occasions. He was brought into court in chains. Many intellectual and professional associates who feared the displeasure of the American government backed away from him.

AKBAR MUHAMMAD

There is an axiom that many of us reference: "Those who fail to learn the lessons of history are doomed to repeat them." In order not to fall victim to this axiom, we must first know history. Too few of us know too little about the history of the great ones who struggled, fought and died that we might stand here today.

Du Bois was a man who was strong enough to change directions as his knowledge and views grew. In early February 1951, after being charged with the failure to register as a foreign agent, a fundraiser was planned at the Essex House Hotel in New York City on his 83rd birthday, February 23, 1951, to help with his trial expenses. Four days before the event, the Essex House Hotel canceled the contract. According to many, he was turned down by most hotels in New York. He finally settled for Small's Paradise in Harlem.

It was painful to read how the NAACP voted in March 1953 not to aid Du Bois in his fight against the unjust indictment handed down by the U.S. courts. This was an organization that he helped found in 1909 and to which he devoted 28 years of his life. Consistently for seven years, the FBI and other government agencies harassed him. They took his passport to keep him from traveling. This also took him away from the international circuit.

Look at the parallels of the history. In 1958, Du Bois took his passport back and went to China, which was an off-limits country, and his passport was taken from him again. Look at the leader of the Nation of Islam, Minister Farrakhan, who is also being harassed by the FBI. His passport was taken for the second time for the same reason they used against Du Bois – he visited an off-limits country. Minister Farrakhan knew that he did not violate any law because, as a publisher of a newspaper, he could visit any off-limits country.

AFRICA AND THE WORLD: REVISITED

In 1960, Du Bois wanted very much to attend the July 1st inauguration of the first president of Ghana, Dr. Kwame Nkrumah. This was three years after Ghana gained its independence from England. Ghana had now become a republic. It was his old friend, Dr. Nkrumah who used his influence as an African leader to get Du Bois' passport reinstated so he could come to Ghana. Du Bois did travel to Accra for the inauguration and it was then that Dr. Nkrumah asked him to relocate there.

In October 1961, Du Bois made his final departure from the United States to Ghana. When his son David's passport expired while in Africa, the U.S. embassy in Cairo refused to reissue it. He traveled to Ghana with his son, where he was issued a Ghanaian passport. Dr. Nkrumah made Dr. Du Bois a citizen of Ghana and called him the "First Citizen of Africa."

There is so much more to the life of this great African. During Black History Month, we should read one of his biographies. On February 23rd as we celebrate our Saviours' Day, we also have the work of this great scholar, struggler, writer, activist and man who would not let the might of America terrorize him to abandon his life's work of fighting for justice for his people.

AKBAR MUHAMMAD

9

Qadhafi's Call for Reparations and a Historic Meeting of African Leaders in Libya

Libyan leader Muammar Qadhafi, during the 4th Extraordinary Meeting of the Organization of African Unity (OAU) and the 30th anniversary of the Libyan Revolution recently held in Libya, called for the West to pay reparations for slavery and damages done to Africa. He also called for a return of all African artifacts robbed by Europeans and others. It was one of the greatest gatherings of African heads of state in the 20th century.

The Honorable Minister Louis Farrakhan, leader of the Nation of Islam, received the only invitation extended to a North American delegation, according to organizers. Minister Farrakhan, who was unable to attend because of health reasons, sent his chief of staff Leonard Farrakhan Muhammad, his son Mustapha Farrakhan, his international representative Akbar Muhammad, and his personal physician Dr. Abdul Alim Muhammad to meet with Colonel Qadhafi. Dr. Alim Muhammad, who is also the Nation of Islam's Minister of Health, gave an in-depth report on Minister Farrakhan's health to the Libyan leader and many other heads of state who were concerned about the Nation of Islam's leader.

The summit included a call for Blacks in the Diaspora to be included in the dialogue for a United States of Africa. This event was a vindication for the Libyan leader who, in the early 80s, had called for a meeting of African leaders. But because of a threat from the West to withhold aid to participating countries, he was not able to get a quorum.

After seven years of sanctions and isolation, centered on the Lockerbie bombing and a negative image of Colonel Qadhafi, he victoriously emerged to host a meeting of 43 African heads of state. These leaders included former heads of state Ahmed Ben Bella of Algeria and Kenneth Kaunda of Zambia, who have been called the wise men of Africa due to their longevity in the struggle of their countries. The other key missing figure, because of his failing health at the time, was Julius Nyerere of Tanzania, now deceased.

The conference began with a parade that featured 32 of the 53 participating African nations. Colonel Qadhafi, dressed in a white uniform decorated with medals, proudly stood at the helm and saluted the various military representatives.

During the deliberations that began in Sirte, Libya the next day, Colonel Qadhafi honored the sons of two great African heroes: Gamal Nkrumah, son of Dr. Kwame Nkrumah, and Roland Lumumba, son of Patrice Lumumba.

Colonel Qadhafi wanted the final resolution to be completed on September 9, 1999, so that this date would indelibly live in the history of Africa as the day these African leaders determined that Africa must be united.

The words of Kwame Ture had to be in the front of the minds of those who heard him speak on college campuses and to organizations throughout America, the Caribbean, Canada, Africa and Europe: "As Africa is my mother, I know that Africa will unite if they are to survive."

10

Africans in the Diaspora and Africans at Home, We Need Each Other

While traveling and writing about Africa and what is happening on this great continent, I have encountered many opinions. I try to deal with people on their various levels and I also try not to be reactionary. However, I could not help but react to an article that appeared on the front page of the *Wall Street Journal*, Wednesday, March 14th, entitled, "Tangled Roots: For African Americans in Ghana, The Grass Isn't Always Greener." Since I have lived in Ghana for 10 years and traveled to many parts of Africa, I must respond to such a derogatory article written by Pascal Zachary.

The *Wall Street Journal* is one of the most conservative newspapers in America from what I know of it. Its focus is business. However, the only business that was highlighted in this article was the establishment of a vegetarian restaurant in the Cape Coast and Elmina area and the adventures of the owner. The writer mentioned that the African American community is drawn to Ghana "by beautiful beaches, tropical climate, low living costs and, most of all, a sense that this historical heart of the slave trade is an ancestral homeland."

I thought it odd for a paper like the *Wall Street Journal* not to have mentioned the Ghanaian stock market, its gold or even its tourism. Perhaps, I thought, it would have at least mentioned that many are interested in the opportunities to conduct business in Africa.

AKBAR MUHAMMAD

Many African Americans have made a conscious decision to move to Africa to escape the blatant, harsh racism that exists in America. Another incentive is the lack of opportunities in America to use their God-given talents and skills that were learned in America. These skills and talents can be very useful on the African continent. I know that the *Wall Street Journal* is not a major voice for the plight of the Black community. However, it is interesting that this point was missed altogether.

The writer talked about malaria. Many of the readers of the article have not studied tropical diseases. Some people only know it as a name – some kind of sickness that you get in the tropics. Zachary mentioned how electric and water supplies are often interrupted. His point, I ascertained, was to list all the reasons that one should not have the desire to travel to Africa, Ghana in particular. The writer mentioned that African Americans are lumped together with White Americans and are called "obruni" or "white" by Ghanaians.

He also mentioned that many Ghanaians see African Americans as arrogant, which is absolutely correct. However, what the writer should have said is that many of the African Americans who are trained, taught and shaped in White America, have taken on the arrogant attitude of the Americans that is seen all over the world. In most countries that you visit (not just developing countries in Latin America, Africa and Asia but also in Europe), Americans are seen as arrogant. Since we have been under the tutelage of White America for more than 400 years, we have also take on the same arrogance. This is why we need Africa as much as Africa needs us.

We have the opportunity to learn some valuable cultural lessons. Our first lesson as African Americans or Africans in the Diaspora should be in humility and cultural nuances. We must also learn something about the continent from which we were snatched. We must critically examine the horrors of slavery. We need to throw off the shackles of the arrogance taught to us by very arrogant slave masters.

AFRICA AND THE WORLD: REVISITED

Those of us who have read the *Wall Street Journal* article may have understood the real message it's trying to convey: It was designed to discourage the movement of Black capital investments in Ghana that would create the kind of financial marriage that is direly needed on the African continent.

The writer also mentioned how Black people are not welcomed in Ghana and are not able to be employed in government jobs. I would like to give the writer a lesson in history. It was Dr. Kwame Nkrumah who was educated in America at Lincoln University in Pennsylvania. He met African Americans and saw the tremendous potential we had to help the African continent move forward. Ghana was the first country that invited African Americans to relocate there, e.g. Maya Angelou, Alice Windom, W.E.B. Du Bois and George Padmore. The list consists of many artists and writers who moved to Ghana in order to escape the racism of America and experience their cultural homeland. Many of these people were invited and embraced by the country.

Similarly, in the past, many artists such as Richard Wright, Dexter Gordon and James Baldwin moved to Paris to be free to create without facing opposition, persecution and suffering because of the color of their skin. Today, African Americans who suffer racism in America could be looking in the future toward Africa as a Promised Land.

Kwame Nkrumah's vision was to get the Africans in the Diaspora who had been taught well by the slave master to run their society. He felt that, if he brought them home, they could eventually run a society that belonged to Black people. In my opinion, this article was designed to discourage, instead of encourage, African Americans or Africans in the Diaspora to participate in the development of Africa at a time when our expertise is needed.

There are points in that article which need to be addressed jointly with the government of Ghana. This is a new experiment for both Ghanaians and African

Americans and we have to work through the problems that arise. Zachary cited how Americans pay for goods and services more at hospitals and slave dungeons. When I moved to Ghana 10 years ago, very few Ghanaians had even been inside the Cape Coast slave dungeons or knew of their history. Now, because of the influence and attractions of Africans in the Diaspora, we have made these sites a place where schoolchildren and many others visit.

If those individuals are concerned about our being charged higher fees, then why don't they seek donations throughout the world for the upkeep of these historical monuments? God has blessed Ghana in the preservation of these tremendous slave dungeons. The dungeons that housed our people, before they were shipped to America to be made into slaves, are still intact.

African Americans can come and visit these historical sites just as the Jews did when they visited Auschwitz to witness the evidence of their suffering during World War II. This visibility and awareness were a result of Black America's pilgrimage to witness the remnants of these horrible atrocities and teach their children the lesson of "never again."

I am disappointed in such an article because it sabotages the wholesome interaction between African Americans and those on the continent. It discourages reparations, business investments and tourism. The potential for growth in Africa is unlimited. If young Black minds, freshly molded from colleges and universities, would just invest some of their time and talents in Africa, we would see Africa's truest potential.

11

BUILDING BRIDGES, BUILDING HOPE AND THE AFRICAN AGENDA 2000

The theme of the 28th PUSH Conference was an excellent theme for the African Agenda 2000. Reverend Jesse Jackson and his staff presented one of the best conferences since his return to Chicago to rebuild PUSH.

There were many highlights of the conference. One that will remain in my heart and mind was his daughter Santita's singing of *To God Be The Glory*. Her singing made my listening to Vice President Al Gore for 48 minutes, trying to get the right cadence in his speech, worthwhile. God has blessed this young woman with a voice that had everyone's mouth open. The smiles that her singing brought to Rev. Jackson's face lifted all the tiredness seen in his brow from his involvement in every aspect of the conference.

What was most important to me was the international luncheon that focused on Africa. The attendance of Africans at all the forums and dinners and the inclusion of Africans on the staff of Rev. Jackson, one from Ethiopia and one from the Gambia, showed that the African Agenda 2000 is playing a major role in our struggle and movement in America. At the luncheon, the "Kwame Nkrumah Award" was a significant step in keeping the bridge between the Black American community and Africa open.

AKBAR MUHAMMAD

I was honored to share the platform with General Abdul Salaam Abubakar, former head of state of Nigeria. The Nigerian community of Chicago was well represented at the luncheon. I feel Rev. Jackson has proven his ability to build bridges to the larger community of America for all colors, races and religions. His recent work of freeing three soldiers in Yugoslavia, which was highlighted at the conference, proved his ability to get the job done.

While Rev. Jackson has the position of Clinton's Special Ambassador for Democracy in Africa, he has and will use this position and his ability to make a meaningful connection between Africans in the Diaspora and those on the continent. This connection must be spiritual, cultural, business, social, and include non-governmental and governmental organizations. All six areas must have linkages. As the descendants of Africa brought out of Mother Africa in the horrors of the slave trade, we must not be marginalized in our desire to do business on the African continent. God blessed the Mormon Church for its new efforts in Africa; however, our churches and religious organizations must not be left out.

Our professionals, such as doctors, lawyers, architects, engineers, health care workers and retired military personnel, must take advantage of the tremendous opportunities that are opened for them on the African continent. We have in America retired military men and women who are giants in their fields; they can offer their experience and expertise to governments in Africa who want to see a more responsible and respected soldier.

Dr. Leon Sullivan has built the bridge and Rev. Jackson has expanded it. Rev. Jackson is building hope that we can make a difference on the African continent; hope that the Black American community can share in the next century, reshaping the future of Africa; hope that this vast, beautiful, rich potentially great continent will benefit its descendants abroad and its children at home.

AFRICA AND THE WORLD: REVISITED

We thank Rev. Jackson and the Rainbow PUSH Coalition family for receiving General Abdul Salaam Abubakar, his wife, children and staff. We again thank Rev. Jackson for receiving Mrs. Jewel Howard Taylor, First Lady of Liberia, and her staff. As the Chairman of the Board of PUSH, Reverend Willie Barrow said, "We did find the 28th National Convention dynamic, informative and entertaining."

AKBAR MUHAMMAD

12

Through The Door of No Return

Now more than ever, African Americans are traveling abroad in search of their ancestral roots. A trip to the West Coast of Africa is not complete unless you visit one of the more well-known slave dungeons. They are Goree Island in Senegal or Cape Coast and Elmina in Ghana.

Ghana, the first independent African country, is celebrating 40 years of freedom from European rule (1957). The Cape Coast Castle and Elmina Castle are the names of the slave dungeons in Ghana. These two structures are the largest slave dungeons in Africa and have remained basically intact. These historical castles give insight to the missing links in the story of the slave trade. While addressing an audience of Black Americans, I recall saying:

> "When you walk through the slave dungeons and see the holding pens where our ancestors were housed before being shipped to the Americas, you walk through history. Nearly all Blacks from the Diaspora are descendants of those who were kidnapped, housed in dungeons and then survived the perilous journey to the Americas. When you stand at the door called "The Door of No Return" and look out at the Atlantic Ocean, you are viewing a part of your history because those who were taken through this door were never known to have returned."

AKBAR MUHAMMAD

For seven years, I have watched delegation after delegation relive this experience. I feel that this experience can make a difference in the lives of Black youth. This will do more than the boot camps that the federal government and some states have set up to send Black youth who have run afoul of the law. It will have a greater impact than the years spent in a prison cell. What young, gifted Black American youth need is focus. A trip to Africa, I believe, can help develop that focus.

Many delegations of Black Americans, young and old, are traveling to Africa for the first time. As I sat in my home in Ghana watching a televised speech by Ghana's President Jerry John Rawlings, I saw a young Black man break down and cry. President Rawlings, who has taken a keen interest in Africans in the Diaspora, touched him with the words he spoke regarding his perception of the role of Blacks in the Diaspora. The young man described what it meant to him to put his foot on African soil for the first time.

I understood his tears and his words of how he wanted to go back to America and make a difference. One cannot walk through the slave dungeons in Africa and not think about the modern dungeons being built in America, known as prisons, jails, correctional facilities, boot camps and juvenile detention centers.

More than 400 years ago, Europeans designed the slave dungeons to warehouse Black men and women destined for lives of bondage in the Western Hemisphere. Two hundred years later, the federal and state governments of the United States are designing prisons to warehouse Black men and women again. The prison population of America is out of control. We must find a way to make every facility of incarceration have "Doors of No Return" for our young men and women.

AFRICA AND THE WORLD: REVISITED

Of the 1.6 million men and women incarcerated in America today (the largest jail population in the world), there are 116,000 female inmates. This has rendered a devastating effect on Black families. Some children have to face the harsh reality that both of their parents may become incarcerated. With the private prison programs (prison as a business), it appears that district attorneys and states have bought shares in these private prison corporations. To protect their investments, they are vigorously working to keep the prisons full.

The Trans-Atlantic Slave Trade is considered the Black Holocaust. The destruction of Black life in the prisons of America is fast becoming the new Black Holocaust. Let us consider whether it is possible for some of these young men and women to build a new reality on the African continent.

AKBAR MUHAMMAD

III
*AFRICA & THE HONORABLE
MINISTER LOUIS FARRAKHAN:
AN INCOMPARABLE BOND*

13
The National Agenda And Africa

At the recent International Convention of the Nation of Islam, the Honorable Minister Louis Farrakhan issued the National Agenda. Dr. Ben Chavis Muhammad, with a staff of eminent thinkers, put together this excellent document with the input from Minister Farrakhan. As I read through this excellent document on a recent flight from Africa, I could not help foreseeing in the books, word after word, what could benefit Americans who are suffering because of leadership that is plagued by vanity, greed, lust for power and an inordinate self-interest. I saw these words and statements good for Africa and African leaders too. My 10 years of working, learning and traveling across Africa have been challenging, rewarding and, yes, painful.

There is talk of the new African leadership. I know firsthand how Western dominating nations pick what they describe as the new crop of African leadership; they call them "responsible" leaders. The first lesson we must learn, as Malcolm X would say, is, "responsible to whom and what?" When your oppressor calls you responsible, they are simply saying you are responsible to them and their establishments.

If you study the stories in the Western press about Africa, you would say, as Minister Farrakhan writes about America, "Africa lies on her deathbed and in dire need of guidance and new direction." There are many African leaders who want to lead and work to help their country and people move forward. However, they are strapped with old baggage and the remains of the dominating nations who push programs and ideas that do not take into consideration the language, history and culture of African people.

AKBAR MUHAMMAD

Look at the headlines out of Africa in the last three months of this new year. The tragic death of 900 men, women and children in Uganda at the hands of mad leaders in a religious cult. The more one reads and hears about this, the angrier one gets. Commentaries on the radio say life is so hard in this part of Africa

that people are joining religious cults with doomsday philosophies. The floods in Mozambique. Twelve million people are at risk of AIDS in South Africa, where a myth was started that purports if you are infected with the HIV virus, you can heal yourself by having sex with a young virgin girl. This baseless practice has resulted in an increase in the rape cases of young girls in South Africa.

As we read through the National Agenda, there is much in it that can be a guiding light for not only those who are suffering from misguided leadership in the United States, but also those who suffer from misguided leadership in other parts of the world. In the age of technology, we can find that we are all connected in one way or another. We hope that not only those in leadership in America will take time to read the National Agenda, but also that our brothers and sisters on the African continent will do the same.

14

Alex Haley Mosque and School To Open in The Gambia

When Alex Haley was working on the biography of Malcolm X, Malcolm encouraged him to trace his roots. Alex pursued this. In the early 1970s, he wrote a letter to Minister Louis Farrakhan, who was then the minister of Muhammad Mosque No. 7 in New York City. In his letter, he said, "Brother Louis, Malcolm was right. I've traced my roots to a small Muslim village of Juffureh in the country Gambia, West Africa." This was the beginning of the classic book, "Roots" that resulted in the television series that was shown throughout the world in many languages.

Before his death, Alex Haley made frequent visits to the village of Juffureh. He had promised the people of the village that he would build a small mosque for them. He gave some funds to the former government of the Gambia. However, the project never got underway, except for a few cement blocks to lay the foundation.

During Minister Farrakhan's most recent world tour, he visited the Gambia. He was encouraged to visit the area where Alex Haley found his roots. Upon seeing what Alex envisioned and wanted to do for the people of this village, Minister Farrakhan made a decision that he would advance the necessary funds to build the mosque and a school.

AKBAR MUHAMMAD

On June 25, 1999 in cooperation with the government of Gambia and His Excellency Dr. Alhaji Yahya, A.J.J. Jammeh (who is said to be the youngest president in the world today at age 34), we will dedicate and open the mosque in Juffureh. Minister Farrakhan, who is still convalescing after his surgery, is sending his wife Khadijah Farrakhan, son Mustapha Farrakhan, and chief of staff Leonard Muhammad to represent him at the opening. Sheikh Hassan Cisse, Grand Imam Tijaniyya of Senegal will deliver the sermon in English and the local languages.

The dedication will open the 4th Annual Roots Festival. The festival's organizing committee has invited members of the African American community to join them for the festival. There will be musical entertainment, symposiums on doing business in Africa and other planned activities.

The Roots Festival Organizing Committee anticipates guests from England, Germany, Africans living in the Scandinavian countries as well as other African countries. There will be a delegation of 60 travelers from America who are friends of Minister Farrakhan and members of the Nation of Islam.

The completion of the mosque in the Gambia is the first building project of the Nation of Islam in Africa. The second project has been started in Ghana, West Africa.

15

Let Farrakhan Have The Money

Brother Muammar Qadhafi of Libya pledged a donation of $1 billion to Minister Farrakhan and the Nation of Islam. The United States government rejected the application for the grant. The question is why. This grant would help the people for whom Minister Farrakhan has spent 42 years of his life working. The government of America, after watching the Nation of Islam for 67 years, knows full well that we are not a terrorist group or organization.

Money Would Help America

Night after night, we watch the local news reporting crimes in the streets of America, mostly in Black communities. Minister Farrakhan has shown how the Nation of Islam can reform young men and women caught up in the vicious web of crime, vice and drugs.

This grant from Brother Qadhafi would help support organizations working for our people and other oppressed Americans. He would use the funds to create jobs in the inner cities. He would give full scholarships to our young students who are out of college and universities because of government cutbacks.

AKBAR MUHAMMAD

Minister Farrakhan has expressed a desire to liberate the nearly 1.2 million Blacks and other minorities in the prisons and jails of America. This program would be according to Point Number 5 in the Muslim Program under *What The Muslims Want*, and Minister Farrakhan's writing on this subject in his book, "Torchlight for America."

Do Your Research

How much money does America give to Israel each year? How much of the taxpayers' money is now going to Russia each year? This grant represents moral and religious issues. Why and how can America stop charity coming from one Muslim brother to another?

Many Black political, religious and civic leaders have problems at times thinking like free men and women. Some feel it is important to think for their former slave masters first. They first want to know how the master feels about Farrakhan, the money and Qadhafi. Only a slave lets his master make up his or her mind for them. If one is truly free, one thinks first in his or her self-interest. I am suggesting a national survey to ask the masses of Black Americans how they feel about Minister Farrakhan receiving this grant from Brother Qadhafi. Then, we can present the results, first to the Black leadership and community, then to the government of America.

Let Us End The War Against Libya

War and sanctions take lives. More than 2,000 Libyans have lost their lives because of the hardships of travel, and thousands more have lost their lives because of medical reasons.

The sanctions were said to have been put in place to force Libya to turn over the two men accused in the tragic bombing of Pan Am Flight 103. Libya has offered to turn them over to a neutral country, but America has rejected this option. The real agenda of the United States government is to keep Libya isolated and stop its foreign policy of helping African nations and Islamic causes, such as the $1 billion grant to Minister Farrakhan and the Nation of Islam. Let Farrakhan have the money!

16

Farrakhan's Africa Trip: Prelude to Million Family March

Fourteen days before the Million Family March, Minister Louis Farrakhan made a surprise trip to Africa, visiting six African nations and one European nation. What was so important that Minister Farrakhan, who was preparing for the historical Million Family March, would leave America on a peace mission to Africa?

During a meeting in Tripoli, Libya in September 2000 with Muammar Qadhafi, the leader of the Libyan Revolution, Qadhafi felt that Minister Farrakhan's input would assist in the peace process in the Democratic Republic of the Congo (DRC), formerly known as Zaire. Minister Farrakhan, who has no personal agenda other than to seek peace between brothers, visited to see if he could give a word of hope to help stop the carnage and waste of resources. Further, Brother Qadhafi felt that the former president of Nicaragua, Daniel Ortega, as well as Minister Farrakhan represented two voices of reason to which the entities in this conflict would respond.

AKBAR MUHAMMAD

The entities involved in the conflict are as follows: Laurent Kabila, head of state of the DRC, President Robert Mugabe of Zimbabwe, President Jose Eduardo dos Santos of Angola, President Yoweri Museveni of Uganda, President Paul Kagame of Rwanda, and President Sam Njoma of Namibia. The problems of the DRC are problems that have now affected all of Africa – from north to south, and east to west. This conflict threatens to destabilize the whole southern region of Africa.

Minister Farrakhan flew to Tripoli, and from there to Senegal to consult with President Abdoulaye Wade. After Senegal, he went to Mali, where President Oumar Konare flew with him to Namibia to consult with President Njoma. After Namibia, he flew to Zimbabwe to consult with President Mugabe, whose wisdom and clarity on conflict shed tremendous light. Mugabe's involvement with 12,000 troops in the Congo has been misrepresented by the Western media due to the media's dislike of him taking land from White farmers and giving it to the indigenous people of Zimbabwe. The U.S. President sent troops to the Congo to keep the recognized, yet threatened, government of President Kabila in place. The DRC was being taken over by forces backed by Uganda and Rwanda. From Zimbabwe, Minister Farrakhan flew to South Africa, and then returned to America.

A solution that Brother Qadhafi offered was a call for a United States of Africa or Union of African States. If this idea could be rapidly pushed forward, it would help end some of the conflicts on the African continent that are remnants of the colonial masters. It will also help eliminate the residue of the Cold War conflicts that were played out on the African continent.

AFRICA AND THE WORLD: REVISITED

The conflict in Central Africa cannot truly be understood by Africans in the Diaspora by reading short news reports, for it is quite complex and involved. Minister Farrakhan clearly articulated to all that he met on this trip that there must be a strong and effective lobby of Africans in the Diaspora to compel our political leaders and the press to project more clarity on the roots of this conflict. The Black American community must become more informed on what is happening on the African continent. Muammar Qadhafi feels that, from inside of America, we can make a difference, especially within the U.S. Congress.

Qadhafi gave clear examples, citing the countries upon which the government of America has either imposed sanctions or threatened to impose sanctions. The sanctions are imposed to make sure that these countries have no economic aid, which only further destabilizes their economies. In addition, the sanctions cause the people of those countries to suffer, simply because of agreements America and other nations have with the leadership of those countries. They are not mindful of the millions of people who are affected by these decisions.

Minister Farrakhan felt strongly that there are many policies implemented by the American government, of which the masses, public officials and servants have no knowledge. He further states that, with the help of Allah (God), this is what we hope to change. The Honorable Minister Louis Farrakhan's plan is to continue to participate in the peace process by exposing and explaining the dynamics involved in these senseless wars in Africa.

AKBAR MUHAMMAD

17

LOUIS FARRAKHAN AT 70: HIS IMPACT

On May 11, 2003, Minister Louis Farrakhan, leader of the Nation of Islam, turned 70 years old. He has had a most interesting life since the early age of six when he began his violin lessons. Maria Farrakhan Muhammad, his second eldest daughter, put together a celebration of his 70th birthday, which launched the Louis Farrakhan Prostate Cancer Foundation.

The event was truly spectacular for those who were fortunate enough to attend the weekend of activities in Chicago. The launch of the foundation included free cancer screenings for all men in attendance. Frankie Beverly of Maze performed an excellent concert tribute to Minister Farrakhan and the foundation.

The highlights of Minister Farrakhan's life were portrayed through film at the dinner gala. The architects of this film were Bill Cherry, John Bellamy and Alif Muhammad. Don Todd, who handled the production end of the weekend, also did an excellent job. The speakers represented Minister Farrakhan's broad base of support from leaders such as the Reverend Jesse Jackson, Tavis Smiley, Cornell West, Beverly Todd and Cliff Kelley, Chicago radio talk show host who was the gala's master of ceremony. Their words of support were befitting of a man who has given 48 of his 70 years to the ministry for the liberation of his people. Minister Farrakhan has been blessed to make an impact in just about every corner of the world.

AKBAR MUHAMMAD

While listening to the words of love and support expressed by his friends and family, I reflected on the years that I journeyed and worked with Minister Farrakhan. There have been many occasions where we have traveled and experienced plenty together.

At the end of April 2003, I returned to America from Africa and a few days later I found myself on a plane bound for the island of Jamaica. As my plane landed in Montego Bay, my mind reflected back 32 years when I made my first trip to this most beautiful island.

The occasion for that trip was to make arrangements for Minister Farrakhan to take a long-needed and well-deserved vacation. The Honorable Elijah Muhammad advised Minister Farrakhan that there were two places where the sun was best for his chest condition – Mexico and Jamaica.

It was after six years of extremely hard work rebuilding the Nation of Islam in New York City. After the assassination of Malcolm X, Muhammad Mosque No. 7 had a credibility problem. At the end of his fifth year in New York, Minister Farrakhan had beaten back most of the lies and half-truths.

His address to the Congress of African People in September 1970, through a strange twist of fate, turned out to be the keynote speech of the conference. This one speech by our champion restored the Nation of Islam's credibility in the liberation community. There was no denying Minister Farrakhan after this. The Honorable Elijah Muhammad highly praised his speech.

AFRICA AND THE WORLD: REVISITED

Minister Farrakhan was not sure that he would be permitted to land and stay in Jamaica because a few years earlier the Jamaican government under then Prime Minister Hugh Sheare rejected the Honorable Elijah Muhammad and his delegation after his plane landed in Jamaica. Under this particular government, the Nation of Islam's mosque meetings and newspaper, *Muhammad Speaks*, were banned. However, Minister Farrakhan was allowed to enter the country, his first trip to Jamaica, the land of his father's birth. The three weeks in Jamaica helped him sharpen his focus and return to America to face the most trying period of his life thus far, 1972-1976.

In 1972, when Michael Manley was elected prime minister, the doors of Jamaica were opened once again to the Nation of Islam, our newspaper and the leadership. Prime Minister Manley hosted a Muhammad Ali Day in December 1974. Again, Minister Farrakhan carried the day, with his address to more than 25,000 people in the national stadium. The word went out that a brother from North America was delivering a message that liberated the minds, hearts and souls of Black people. Minister Farrakhan's message not only impacted all of Jamaica, but the whole Caribbean and beyond.

Who would have pictured the son of Caribbean parents who, at 22, joined the Nation of Islam (1955); at 32, was moved from Boston to New York (1965); at 42, watched the Nation fall (1975); at 52, was pushed in the national spotlight, trying to help Reverend Jesse Jackson in his run for president (1985); and at 62, led the historic Million Man March where nearly two million men responded to his call (1995).

The Honorable Louis Farrakhan at 70 – the life of this noble son of Africa and his impact on America, the Caribbean, Africa and the world must be told and recorded in volumes of books.

AKBAR MUHAMMAD

IV

AFRICA & AKBAR: SENTIMENTS ALONG MY JOURNEY

Muhammad Ali with Akbar Muhammad, Washington University in St. Louis (1975)

18

DEATH OF MOBUTU

When I picked up the newspaper and read of the death of Joseph Mobutu Sese Seko, former president of the Democratic Republic of the Congo (Zaire) on Sunday, September 7, 1997, I could not help thinking about a book written in the 1970s entitled, "The Tragedy of Lyndon B. Johnson." When Mobutu attended school in Brussels, the Belgians began to cultivate him as a person who would report to his "master." The tragedy is that where he started is where he ended. When the master had no more use of his services, Mobutu was cast to the side like a used shoe.

I first met him in Cairo, Egypt at the 30th anniversary of the Cairo Conference Center. He looked like a man who was looking for friends. The CIA and the West were finished with him by this time. My second and last encounter with Mobutu was in Tripoli, Libya. He had come to the country of an African leader who supported most of the opposition against him. My meeting with him was soon after the Million Man March that took place on October 16, 1995 in Washington, D.C. Mobutu had seen the event on television. He commented in French, calling it a great demonstration. I gave him a gift of a Million Man March t-shirt. Then, he asked about the possibility of Minister Louis Farrakhan visiting his country.

During his historic World Friendship Tour, Minister Farrakhan did stop in the Democratic Republic of the Congo (Zaire). Our plane flew into Gbadolite and we drove from Mobutu's private airport to his residence. It happened to be the same home from which Mobutu fled in May 1995 as Kabila's rebel army advanced on Gbadolite.

AKBAR MUHAMMAD
The Death of Patrice Lumumba

When the West heard the inauguration speech of newly elected Prime Minister Patrice Lumumba of the Democratic Republic of the Congo (Zaire) on June 30, 1960, the wheels were set in motion to eliminate him. It was CIA Director Allen Dulles who feared this charismatic and dynamic young man because he had a vision that was in the best interest of the people of the Congo and not Belgium, France or the United States.

Subsequently, the new prime minister was brutally murdered. The fact that the CIA under Allen Dulles ordered Lumumba's assassination came to light in 1975 at a United States Senate Committee hearing investigation into the assassination plot against Lumumba. The murder was directed through a CIA operative – Joseph Mobutu.

It was Mobutu and his troops, with the aid of the CIA in Kinshasa (formerly Leopoldville), who assisted in the capture of Lumumba on December 1, 1960. It was Mobutu, under the direction of his new boss, the CIA, who turned Lumumba over to his bitter enemy Moise Tshombe to be killed on January 17, 1961.

In his book, "The CIA: A Forgotten History," William Blum writes that, in September 1960 the CIA sent one of its scientists, Joseph Schneider, to the Congo carrying lethal biological material (a virus) specifically intended for use in Lumumba's assassination. The book goes on to say that the virus, which was supposed to produce a fatal disease indigenous to the Congolese region in Africa, was transported in a diplomatic pouch. The body of Lumumba was driven around for days in the trunk of a CIA agent's car while they contemplated its most effective disposal.

AFRICA AND THE WORLD: REVISITED

Did Mobutu Do Any Good?

When one looks back at the 31 years of Mobutu as the head of state in the Congo, it is challenging to find a positive legacy because of his well-known evil deeds. However, we must give this man credit for changing the names of cities and the country from the names given by the colonial masters, such as Leopoldville to Kinshasa and Stanleyville to Kisangani.

I would like to see the leaders of South Africa and Namibia change the names of their capitals from Johannesburg and Windhoek to names that represent Africa and not Europe. Also, Mobutu was able to bring what was one of the greatest fights in the history of boxing to Africa, "The Rumble in the Jungle" between Muhammad Ali and Joe Frazier. He encouraged the people of the Congo to use their African names with pride.

Mobutu's immortal lifestyle can serve as a lesson to Black leaders not only on the African continent but throughout the world. It is described in a verse from the Muslim religious text, the Holy Qur'an, Chapter 14, verse 22:

> *"And the devil will say when the matter is decided: surely God promised you a promise of truth and I promised you, then failed you."*

AKBAR MUHAMMAD

19

A Special Ramadan For The People of Libya

For the last 10 years, faith and circumstances have had me traveling outside of America during the Muslim fasting month of Ramadan. This year, people in America and the West got a full ear about the fast, which started in December. President Bill Clinton's bombing attack, four days before the beginning of the fast, caused news reports to focus on the fast. The press, as well as the rest of the world, wanted to know if Clinton would continue the untimely bombing during the holiest period of the Muslim year. Better judgment would have him stop the bombing just before the fast began. More than likely, his advisers told him that the anger of approximately 1.4 billion Muslims would be turned on the United States and Great Britain if they continued to attack at the beginning of the fast.

Last year, during Minister Farrakhan's third historical World Friendship Tour, we spent the last nine days of Ramadan in Saudi Arabia. We flew to Russia and prayed the Eid prayers (the celebration at the end of the 30-day fast) with Russian Muslims. It was a glorious and remarkable sight to see nearly 15,000 Muslims praying inside and outside the mosque in Moscow. Those outside made their prayers in the cold and snow of the Russian winter.

This year, near the closing days of the fast, I was in Libya. One would think that, after seven years of unjust sanctions, the Libyan people would be suffering from shortages of goods in their market. You would also expect to find some gloom among the people because they have been unable to bring closure to the sanctions that have plagued their nation.

On the contrary. I found the markets overflowing with goods from around the world and a genuine spirit among the people, especially after Iftar (the breaking of the fast). At night, the streets of Tripoli were alive with activity. You could see families shopping with their children in anticipation of the Eid. It is a time of gift-giving and a three-day holiday throughout the Muslim world.

As I walked among the people, I found the warmth of holiday-type festivities that most Westerners experience during the Christmas season. At night, the mosques were filled to capacity with people praying. You could feel that this year (1999) will be a special year for the Libyan people.

On September 1, 1999, Libya will celebrate the 30th year of the Libyan Revolution, which changed the quality of its people's lives for the better. The Libyan leadership under Muammar Qadhafi used the blessing of oil wealth for the benefit of the Libyan masses. This wealth was used in the areas of education, medicine and national development. Also, thousands of Libyans were sent abroad to be trained in all fields of higher education.

The fast of Ramadan is always taken very seriously in Libya. This year, the Libyan brothers and sisters said that the fasting period of 1998-1999 has a special meaning because of the anticipation of the celebration of 30 years of struggle and the expected lifting of unjust sanctions by Western nations.

20

The Untimely Death of Earl T. Shinhoster ...

His Struggle Must Continue

I feel a great sense of loss and pain over the death of my brother and friend Earl T. Shinhoster of Atlanta, Georgia. Earl served the NAACP for 35 years. At the time of his death, he was its National Field Secretary and National Director of Voter Empowerment and Coordination. He also served as chairman of the Georgia delegation for the National Summit on Africa. Earl died in a tragic accident on Sunday, June 11, 2000 just outside of Montgomery, Alabama. He died the way he lived his life – helping and serving.

When Earl believed in something, he selfishly gave of himself. He was a visionary who approached his work with dedication and passion. He had a great love for Africa and was committed to connecting Africans in the Diaspora with Africans on the continent of Africa. This connection was something in which Earl believed. He enthusiastically agreed to assist me in coordinating a U.S. tour for the First Lady of Liberia, Mrs. Jewel Howard Taylor and a delegation of government ministers. Earl had a full plate of responsibilities, however he thought that Liberia and her plight were important, and that our communities would benefit from firsthand, direct dialogue.

AKBAR MUHAMMAD

In preparing for a 10-city tour for the Liberian delegation, I asked my daughter Samimah Aziz to return to America from Africa to coordinate the project. She agreed and was in the vehicle with Earl when the accident occurred. Also injured in the accident was Ademah Hackshaw, the network news producer and coordinator for the Georgia leg of the tour.

Earl's wife Ruby Shinhoster and his son Michael Omar showed great strength at the funeral. The words from Earl's youngest sister comforted us all and gave a vivid picture of his committed soul. First Lady Taylor read a statement from the Liberian government by order of the president. The communique read in part:

- That Earl Shinhoster is made a citizen of Liberia postmortem
- That the family of Earl Shinhoster will be given land in Liberia
- That a foundation will be established and named in honor of Earl T. Shinhoster
- That the foundation will be named The Earl T. Shinhoster People to People for Africa Foundation

I know that there is nothing we can do to replace the void felt in the lives of Ruby and Michael Omar. We pray and ask God for guidance and mercy. Earl came forth and lost his life working and helping in a cause in which he believed. Let us not allow his death to stop what he hoped for and envisioned.

The best way that I can say thank you to my brother and his family is to make sure that his work continues. It was my daughter Samimah (now recovering in a hospital in Montgomery) who created the idea of a People to People network, a campaign to inform American communities, businesses, government and individuals about the needs, revitalization efforts and natural resources in Liberia. Minutes before the fatal accident, Earl, Samimah and Ademah were having a discussion about methods and strategies for developing Liberian investments and philanthropic relationships in America.

AFRICA AND THE WORLD: REVISITED

I am asking all who knew Earl Shinhoster or share the passion of his work, and those who know Samimah, to help us continue in the process for peace and understanding in Africa.

AKBAR MUHAMMAD

21

Diana Ross, Wake Up and Smell The Coffee

What Diana Ross suffered traveling from London Heathrow Airport back to America is not unusual for Black people to experience when traveling, especially Africans and Black Americans. What Diana refuses to realize or say is, "I feel like a victim of racism."

Diana Ross is known throughout the world. For the airport staff to take her bags and search through her personal belongings, as if she was some common criminal, was totally unnecessary. It was done to humiliate her and further say that we are going to treat you like we treat all other niggers.

I have been traveling throughout Europe and there is a new movement in Europe that is reflected in theirtreatment of Black people. You see it at the airport in Italy. When a plane arrives from an African country, Africans are sent through a special door and given a little card. When they go through security control, their passports are carefully inspected to see if they are forged. They are asked what is their next destination. Their visas are examined. And they are addressed in a very rude manner.

When you get off a plane coming from an African country in Amsterdam, there are security people at the gate who stop every African to look at their passport, examine their visas and ask them where they are going. Yet, they wave White passengers right through.

Diana Ross refused, on Larry King's show, to say the incident had anything to do with race. It was obvious that, if the woman checked Diana twice and said, "I'm doing my job," and then proceeded to rub her hands all over Diana's body again, she was telling Diana Ross, "Look, you are Black and you have some nerve questioning me. I'm White and I'm in charge here and I will do it again."

But Diana Ross, who is lost from herself, needs to reexamine how she views the world. She has a very Eurocentric view of the world and refuses to see racism as it is. For the British airport police to take her to a police station, go through her bags and put her in a room, as if she were some common criminal, was racial harassment. She is Diana Ross. Would they have done the same to Cher, Mariah Carey or Celine Dion?

22

My Ali Story

I, like thousands of people in America, have an Ali story: how he touched our lives, inspired us and, in many cases, changed the course of our lives. He touched people near and far. Many never had an opportunity to see Muhammad Ali in person, but through books, documentaries and his movie roles, many came to know him. There were many who did not like Muhammad Ali. Some thought that he was brash and arrogant. They were hoping that someone would defeat him in the ring or that he would suffer blows to mess up his "pretty face."

Two days after his death, the *New York Times* described Ali in a way that made readers think aboutthe impact he had, not only in America but throughout the world. The headlines read, "From Blockbuster Fighter to the Country's Conscience" and "The Champ Who Transcended Boxing."

Growing up and watching Ali (we happen to be the same age), I can say with certainty that he probably saved the lives of hundreds of thousands of young Americans who would have went to fight in the tragic, unholy Vietnam War – a war that took 58,000 precious American lives. Had Ali not protested, we may have lost more than 100,000 lives in Vietnam. Given Ali's courageous stand not to go to war, he inspired and encouraged others to stand down and say no to war.

AKBAR MUHAMMAD

His insight and political position were rooted in the fact that, at 22 years of age, he accepted the Teachings of the Honorable Elijah Muhammad, leader of the Nation of Islam. What he learned as a young Muslim not only sharpened his focus and determination in the ring, but it also opened up his mind to the condition of Black people in America. He spoke out about discrimination and demanded social justice.

As the news unfolds about Muhammad Ali, we see many trying to sidestep and minimize his deep involvement in the Nation of Islam and the commitment he made to his faith. His stand not to go to Vietnam pricked the country's conscience, as mentioned in the *New York Times*.

When he was given the name Muhammad Ali, it made those who followed boxing in America and throughout the world know immediately that there was something different about this fighter. When he won the championship from Sonny Liston (when most who followed boxing thought that there was no way an untried youngster could beat a man they thought was invincible), he pumped new life into boxing. Ali created a dynamic where boxers would now make the millions of dollars that they rightly deserved.

I was blessed to be in Muhammad Ali's company many times. I was blessed to be in charge of the Shabazz Restaurant in New York, which prepared Muhammad Ali's food when he fought at Madison Square Garden. I was blessed to be in Turkey when Muhammad Ali was invited to visit Turkey on his first visit by the then foreign minister. Again, the *New York Times* was correct. He was a champion who transcended the boxing ring.

Many would like to see Muhammad Ali as a man who crossed the bridge that got him over to the other side, and then turned and cursed the bridge. He was a Muslim and many would like to take that away from him and make him just a good American who had a tremendous ability to fight. Long live the courageous spirit of Muhammad Ali!

V
AFRICA & THE WORLD: GLOBAL AGENDAS

AKBAR MUHAMMAD

Minister Louis Farrakhan, Abdul Sharrieff Muhammad, Imam Adbul Malik, Akbar Muhammad in Saudi Arabia

23
Can Western-Style Democracy Benefit Africa?

Can the African world rely on Western-style democracy to be the voice of the people for true democratic reforms, free and fair elections? While observing the elections in Ghana, a stable country, I noticed that there were virtually no problems. At least they were very small compared to the ones America faced in its recent presidential elections.

I also observed enormous amounts of resources spent on campaigning, posters, buses, radio and television advertisement, travel, rallies, billboards, t-shirts, caps, buttons, trucks, free food, etc. I thought about how many children's school fees could have been paid; how many hospitals could have been built; how many businesses could have been started; how many low-cost houses could have been built; and how many hospital bills could have been paid.

When you look at an array of candidates running for one office and the resources that are spent to make that happen, it will not diminish; It will only increase as time goes on. Is this the way for Africa?

I do not want anyone to think that I am advocating a dictatorship or one-party system with a dictator who stays in power for 30 years. But we need an alternative to the Western system imposed on us by Europeans and Americans. Their systems that we have adopted have been miserable failures in most countries all over Africa. Is this the way to go for the future of Africa? Or should we look for a system of government that is, yes, a democratic one, but more conducive to our environment, culture and terrain?

What is so bad is that the candidates begin to personally attack each other and their programs. This becomes very vicious. How do you explain to a young child that a candidate is corrupt or stole money? What do you say to a child who is trying to understand that this corrupt person is aspiring to head a government, and you just called him a thief? Dirty politics is the way of the Western world, but it does not have to be the way of Africa.

Following the Westernized system of democracy, trying to use the American or British system to govern African countries and societies, in the long run, will lead Africa straight to hell. You can see some of the results in Africa, even today.

If we condemn the Western system, then we are obligated to come up with a system that speaks more directly to the needs of the African people.

24

LIBYA, FRANCE AND AMERICA: THE AFRICAN AGENDA

After witnessing President Bill Clinton's trip to Africa, many wonder what is the United States' agenda for Africa? The new scramble for Africa has taken a twist that is hard for many to conceive. There is a battle among three countries over which one will influence Africa; only one of the three battling countries is an African nation – Libya.

The West would like to put Libya in the non-African category. This isolation of Libya through sanctions has not stopped Muammar Qadhafi and the Libyan people from pushing forward on their African agenda.

France wants to maintain its influence over the 23 French-speaking African nations as well as establish itspresence in the English- and Portuguese-speaking nations. France is also taking advantage of the American-led sanctions against Libya, Nigeria and the Sudan. France is doing whatever is necessary to make the French presence felt.

Important aspects of President Clinton's trip were to establish the American presence and say to France that America will establish itself to seek its place in the so-called "African Renaissance." With 40 million descendants of Africa in America, President Clinton's actions suggest that America has a vested interest in the future of Africa and that America will be involved in events happening on the African continent.

Qadhafi feels that the two non-African nations are not sincere in their involvement in Africa and that as outsiders they would like to bury any Pan-African thought among current leaders. America and France would like to drive a wedge between the Arab and Islamic North and the rest of the continent. These two predominately White and non-African nations are playing all four cards: race, religion, color and terrorism. America and France are fighting each other over influence in Africa, promising African leaders and the people of Africa that they will do more for their nation if they keep Libya out!

With six years of sanctions, the Libyans have not gotten on their knees to America and the West, but Libyans have struggled through this difficult period, continuing to push their foreign policy objectives. Brother Qadhafi has traveled to other African countries and received many African leaders. The most recent leader received was President Blaise Compaore from Burkina Faso, who will take over the reins of the Organization of African Unity at the annual meeting this year in Ouagaobugou, the capital of Burkina Faso.

Among those African leaders who recently made the very difficult trip to visit Brother Qadhafi was President Laurent Kabila from the Democratic Republic of the Congo; President Nelson Mandela, who made two trips to Libya; President Bakili Muluzi of Malawi; President Zine el-Abidine Ben Ali of Tunisia; President Idriss Deby of Chad; President Charles Taylor of Liberia; President Yahya Jaameh of the Gambia; President Alpha Oumar Konare of Mali; and President Yoweri Museveni of Uganda.

AFRICA AND THE WORLD: REVISITED

The support received by these African leaders shows that, despite the attempts to isolate and demonize Libya and Qadhafi, his influence in Africa remains substantial. Libya has just completed a beautiful hospital in Porto Novo, Benin. Brother Qadhafi sent a top delegation for its opening. His embassy in South Africa is open. Libya has one of the few embassies that exist in the Comoros Islands.

Last year, he flew his planes to Niger and Nigeria, where he spoke to more than 2 million people in Kano. On Friday, May 1st, the first day of the Muslim New Year, he performed a public jumu'ah prayer in N'Djamena, the capital of Chad, where more than 800,000 people attended the sermon. It was attended by President Ange-Felix Patasse of the Central Africa Republic, along with the President of Chad. At the time of this writing, Brother Qadhafi is on his way to Cairo, Egypt.

Since his revolution on September 1, 1969, he was invested with, and supported, many of the leaders who are now in power in Africa. Three of the six countries visited by President Clinton are those that were helped by Brother Qadhafi and the Libyan people. His support, in some cases, was the overriding factor in stabilizing their new regimes.

One hundred fourteen years after the Berlin Conference (1884), the battle for Africa continues…

AKBAR MUHAMMAD

25

The Impact of America's Tragedy on the Nations of Africa

Many Americans are being educated about the religion of Islam as a result of the terrible tragedy that has befallen America. This event will also affect Africa as well. How is Africa responding, since half of its population (approximately 800 million people) is Muslim and believers in the religion of Islam?

In my travels throughout Africa, I was amazed to learn that in the Democratic Republic of the Congo (DRC, formerly Zaire) there are more than 10 million Muslims. [The Imam of Kinshasa has the last name Lumumba.] Throughout Africa, there are Muslim communities of sizable numbers. For instance, in Liberia, Togo, Benin, Cameroon, Central African Republic, Gabon and now in Namibia and Botswana, there are growing numbers of Muslims. The Head of State Bakili Muluzi of Malawi, which has a tremendous Muslim community, is a Muslim.

These facts are unknown to our people. News reports from Uganda this week said that the people in Kampala were selling pictures of Osama bin Laden. The authorities clamped down on them. In the country of Somalia, this has taken place in the streets of Mogadishu.

The language we use to handle the war on terrorism is important for the government of America and its people. The hearts of the leadership of Africa and the masses of its people go out to those who lost loved ones in the terrible attack on the World Trade Center in New York. However, we must not allow the language from some of the ill-informed leaders in this campaign to incite animosity in the nearly 400 million African Muslims against America. They must tailor their language so that it does not appear to be an attack on Islam. In Nigeria, a daily newspaper called *This Day*, warned against "fanning the flames of racial and religious hatred."

During this campaign against terrorism, I began to hear that the tragic deaths of American soldiers in Somalia were charged to Osama bin Laden. If we look at Somalia, it is another country where America had an opportunity to do good, but they abandoned the country.

When a country is stripped of everything, there is no central government or court of law. When people are hungry, the only thing they can turn to is their God. When all hope was lost for the people of Somalia, they simply began to turn to their God and asked Allah to help them to live by the dictates of the Qur'an. They were only seeking a way out of the terrible tragedy that had befallen their country. If they are found turning back to their religion, calling on God and trying to obey the law of their Holy Book, we should not ascribe Somalia the stain of becoming an Islamic fundamentalist state under the influence of Osama bin Laden. We should look at it for what it really is.

An article recently appeared in *The Economist* magazine entitled, "Islam Influence Increasing in Somalia." The influence of Islam has always been among the people of Somalia who were Muslims. However, when the people chose to leave a secular position and return to a spiritual way of life in hopes of finding relief by striving to obey the laws of God, it's inaccurate to put the label of extremist or fundamentalist upon them just because they want to live by Sharia law.

AFRICA AND THE WORLD: REVISITED

The impact of the attack on America has affected every African nation. Many of these nations depend on aid from America, and when America has put up $40 million to deal with the war and rebuilding effort, then quite naturally many African nations will suffer. Their natural inclination is to become more self-reliant. They will look for a spiritual quality to be the driving force to save their society.

Therefore, half of Africa's population, which believes in Islam, will begin to turn more to their faith and themselves instead of hoping that donor nations will pull them out of their misery. It is wrong for America to use money as a weapon to say that, if you join me in this war, I will help you with aid.

President George Bush made some mistakes in his language when this campaign against terrorism was started. The theme was first termed "Infinite Justice." The Muslim world said that only Allah can disperse infinite justice. Then, he said it was the "crusade" against terrorists. Again, the Muslim world said that, if you use the word "crusade," then you play into the hands of certain Muslims who see the West, not on a crusade against terrorists, but against Islamic people throughout the world.

Next, it was said that it is a fight for freedom. Again, this is another bad choice of language. The fight against the individuals who attacked New York and Washington in this terrible tragedy is not a fight for freedom. It is a fight against the people who are described as terrorists and have an agenda.

In the struggle, language is very important. If you are not careful, the language that we will eventually begin to hear from the people of the West, who are only growing in the knowledge of Islam and the Islamic world, is that the Islamic world is not a free world. The people of Africa are listening to the language.

AKBAR MUHAMMAD

26

America's War! Is Africa The Next Target?

Africa, a continent of nearly 800 million people, has a population where 50 percent are Muslims. Islam is growing in Africa at a phenomenal rate. Islamic communities do not have the kind of propagation machine that other religions have on the African continent. Nevertheless, the religion of Islam does seem to grow daily in converts.

The next target in the war against terrorism may be a country or countries in Africa that are predominately Islamic. With the focus on Somalia and the Sudan, there is an indication that Africa may play a role in the next move in the war against terrorism. War strategy and logic demand that, after the destruction of the Taliban and the Al-Qaeda network, the war efforts will need a second quick and easy victory. Iraq may be more difficult than anticipated.

By all indications of the press, on the short list are Somalia, the Sudan and Yemen. On a longer list, there is Libya, Liberia and the Revolutionary United Front (RUF) in Sierra Leone. A wild card could be Zimbabwe in the fight against so-called terrorism; the U.S. could say that Black people who are trying to reclaim their land stolen by Whites are terrorizing White farmers and President Robert Mugabe is at the head of this.

Mr. Walter Kansteiner, assistant secretary of state for African affairs, was recently in Africa to visit four countries. The guarded press reports said he was in Africa in connection with America's fight against terrorism. Washington has hinted that they may spare the Sudan and Libya if they get on their knees and become "good boys." However, they must also give up information that will help America in its war effort. Otherwise, they are threatening that, what they see in Afghanistan may be coming to them soon.

The *Wall Street Journal* stated that America does not want this war to appear like a war against Islam. It stands to reason that this may be why countries like North Korea and Colombia are being mentioned as possible targets. And for good measure, the Philippines has been thrown in as well.

Somalia

Even though the government of Somalia is not stable, it is one of the strategic positions in Africa. Somalia does not have oil or other mineral riches that are considerations in geopolitics. However, Somalia is located on the Horn of Africa. America also has not forgotten the 19 U.S. soldiers who were lost before they pulled out. It is described now as a country where Osama bin Laden had many contacts and some supporters.

During the years of the Cold War, Somalia was considered a coveted prize between the former Soviet Union and the United States. The question was always, who was going to control Somalia? Whoever controlled her would control the Gulf of Aden and entry into the Indian Ocean, which facilitates the movement of cargo ships and oil tankers through the Red Sea and in and out of the Suez Canal. Yemen also has been discussed as a country that may be targeted because of its strategic position.

AFRICA AND THE WORLD: REVISITED

Sudan

The Sudan is a country with the largest land area in Africa. It is strategic because it borders nine countries and now has a tremendous oil reserve. America, being the number one oil junkie in the world, wants to get a hit on the fine oil now found in the Sudan. The recent problems and attempted coup in the Central African Republic revolved around the fact that it borders the Sudan and the coup makers were said to be financed by outside entities. More than likely, President Ange Feliz Patasse's relationship with Libya and Chad is at the root of the problems he is now facing. We can also take into account that Osama bin Laden lived in the Sudan and helped them build many of their roads and major construction projects. He also helped some of the members of the Muslim Brotherhood in the Sudan expand their business enterprises.

Libya, Liberia, Sierra Leone and Egypt

Other countries in Africa are on the "hit list" under the veil of fighting terrorism. Libya is an old story. Most people know that pressure is being put on Muammar Qadhafi as well as Omar al-Bashir, president of the Sudan, to bow down to America. Liberia and Sierra Leone were recently mentioned in a *Washington Post* press report that stated bin Laden was financing his organization with diamonds from the RUF in Sierra Leone. It was reported that the RUF was supported by President Charles Taylor of Liberia; the implication is that Liberia and Sierra Leone were helping finance bin Laden and the Al-Qaeda network.

Sanctions were placed on Liberia long before the attack on America. These sanctions made it difficult for government officials to travel and for ordinary Liberians to obtain visas for travel to countries outside of Africa. When the movement of government officials is restricted, it Is designed to create dissatisfaction within them, with the hope that it will flow down and affect ordinary citizens. Ultimately, this will make it difficult to conduct government or private business when it necessitates travel to Western nations (in particular America).

I believe that, if the American government really was concerned with funds coming to bin Laden, they would have targeted Saudi Arabia to cut him off. That is where the money is coming from.

Also on the longer list of African nations that may be under attack is Egypt; not the government of Hosni Mubarak but the strong Islamic groups that see Mubarak bowing down to America. They feel that his relationship to America is un-Islamic and unprincipled, and he is only taking this position to keep U.S. aid flowing to Egypt. For without it. the economy of Egypt would be in shambles.

As long as Muslims (half of the population across Africa) continue to see innocent people being killed in this bombing campaign during the month of Ramadan, their dislike for America will continue to bolster. African people have shown a love for the American people but no love for Washington's foreign policy. The tourism dollars upon which many African nations have become dependent are drying up because of this war. This does not generate additional love for America; on the contrary, it creates a problem.

In Ghana, tourist dollars become the third largest foreign cash earner for the people, creating many jobs. This summer will be the test period to determine whether the same numbers of Black Americans and Africans in the Diaspora will bring their tourist dollars to African nations.

27

THE PALESTINIAN STRUGGLE: AFRICA CAN MAKE A DIFFERENCE

African leaders should reflect on the axiom, "Those who fail to learn the lessons of history are doomed to repeat them." They should understand who are their true friends and enemies. When the Black people of South Africa were under the vicious, racist apartheid regime, we looked for the support of the entire civilized world to side with the Black masses.

Third World nations, particularly Arab and Muslim countries, immediately responded. Support by the so-called civilized world came too late. We, Africans at home and abroad, expected that corporations would not conduct business with South Africa under its then-apartheid rulers. We condemned Black entertainers who performed in South Africa. We also condemned any African, Caribbean, Asian or Arab government that had diplomatic relations with South Africa at that time.

One of the reasons that the late Jonas Savimbi (recently killed in an ambush in Angola) was never accepted by Black Americans and our leadership was because he was supported by the racist apartheid regime in South Africa. In 1986, President Ronald Reagan, after meeting with Savimbi in the White House, tried to sell him to some uninformed Black leaders as a freedom fighter. Reagan did not succeed.

AKBAR MUHAMMAD

The liberation struggles throughout Africa were, among other things, a fight for land that was taken from them by European settlers. Europeans made imperialism the order of the day everywhere in Africa, Asia and the Middle East. The first stage of the struggle against imperialism produced a national movement in just about every country where European imperialists had established their rule.

Black Nationalism emerged as a natural and necessary reaction to European imperialism and it was effectively used as a rallying cry to rid Africa of foreign control and domination. The common bond in the struggle between Africans on the mainland and Palestinians against White invaders and usurpers made it easy for most of the progressive African states to break diplomatic relations with Israel in the aftermath of Israel's military aggression and occupation of additional Arab lands in 1967.

It was clear to African leaders that imperialism and Zionism have one objective – to clear the land of its native inhabitants. To justify their thefts of the land, imperialists on the African continent called their illegal and cruel acquisitions of land, "The White Man's Burden." In the case of Palestine, Zionists invoked God's name, claiming that thousands of years ago God gave this land to them which belonged to the ancient Canaanites. Their position implies that the God of Israel, unlike the God of the human family, seems to make unjust distinctions among His children.

An African Union Inaugural Summit is scheduled to convene in Pretoria, South Africa in July 2002. The newly formed African Union, which emerged from the Organization of African Unity (OAU) Summit held in Lusaka, Zambia in July 2001, is expected – despite the enormous pressures exerted by Washington – to express solidarity with the Palestinian people and support for a free and independent Palestinian state on Palestinian land currently occupied by the Zionists in violation of United Nations resolutions. African leaders will have a historical opportunity to make their former colonial masters take note that Africa, which was aided by the Arabs during its wars of liberation, has not forgotten the lessons of history.

AFRICA AND THE WORLD: REVISITED

Of all the African leaders, President Thabo Mbeki should understand how pressure by the African masses as well as African leadership could make a difference. What if, in the agreement between the African National Congress (ANC) and the racist apartheid regime of South Africa, it was stated that nearly one million or more Black South Africans could not return to their land? Would that be acceptable?

All African nations should recall how the Palestinian brothers and sisters were granted honorary membership in the OAU. They attended most of the OAU meetings and strongly supported our struggle to free our lands and people.

What if every nation that has opened or reopened a new Israeli embassy (many under American pressure) would recall their ambassadors in protest against the Israeli occupation of Palestinian land, the imprisonment of Yasser Arafat in his Ramallah headquarters and the destruction of the Palestinian Authority's offices in Ramallah and Gaza? The recall of African ambassadors could also be in protest of the Vice President of America going to Israel and clearly showing the world that the American administration, under President George Bush, is extremely biased toward the Israeli side in this war.

African nations can make a difference. The leadership must be principled; they must not fear the loss of aid from America or Israel if Prime Minister Ariel Sharon continues his terror campaigns of assassinations, the targeting of Palestinian leaders and the killing of children. It is clear that Ariel Sharon's policies are failing and producing more suicide bombers.

The next step would be for the African nations, representing nearly 800 million people, to close all Israeli embassies at one time on the African continent. This would open the way for strong African leadership to challenge the Arab world and the oil-producing exporting countries (OPEC) to call for an oil boycott of 30 days or more.

AKBAR MUHAMMAD

The lessons of history must be remembered. The military superiority of America in Vietnam and the French military might in Algeria mattered little against a people driven by a belief in their own causes for national liberation. The Israelis are learning this lesson the hard way.

VI
AFRICA & THE PRESS:
CORRECTING THE DISTORTED LENS OF MULTIMEDIA PROPAGANDA

AKBAR MUHAMMAD

Maxine Waters, Robert Johnson, Akbar Muhammad, Charles Rangel visit to Accra Ghana March 23, 1998

28

Media Coverage and the Fifth African/ African American Summit Conference

As I sat and listened to the closing address at the Fifth African/African American Summit Conference that took place in May, I was moved by Dr. Leon Sullivan, a man who is 72 years old and has such a spirit and exhibits brilliant clarity of mind in his speech. If I had to title his speech that afternoon at the closing, I would call it, "I See No Alps." He very eloquently described Hannibal's army as they left North Africa and crossed over into Europe. On their march to Rome, they had to cross the Alps. Hannibal's army stopped, awed by the majesty of the Alps. One of the generals in the army then turned to the troops and said, "I see no Alps." The army moved forward to cross the Alps.

Dr. Sullivan used this picture to talk about how people see Africa and some of the problems that have been portrayed by the Western media about Africa – the problems of Sierra Leone, the Eritrea-Ethiopia conflict, Somalia's problems, the ongoing civil war in the Sudan, and the fighting now waging in the Democratic Republic of the Congo (formerly Zaire). We hear about new outbreaks of violence in Congo Brazzaville, the problem that Uganda is now facing, and the rumbling in Liberia. This is the extent of what is reported in the Western media.

AKBAR MUHAMMAD

However, Africa is a huge continent and it is a continent with so much potential. Since 1991, with his first summit conference in Cote d'Ivoire, Dr. Sullivan has made a courageous effort to build bridges, and then create movement back and forth across those bridges between Africans in the Diaspora and those on the continent.

Judging from what I know and what I have heard of the last four summits, I would say that the fifth conference held in Ghana was the best. I do not say this because I live in Ghana or am trying to stroke President Jerry Rawlings and his staff, which is led by Kwesi Ahwoi on the Ghana side and Cecil Perkins on the American side. The conference sent a clear message that the time is now for Africans in the Diaspora and those at home to focus on each other. It took a little over 400 years and a lot of pain, suffering and death for us to come to the conclusion that all we have is each other.

During one of the three speeches delivered by Reverend Jesse Jackson at the conference, he made a point about the absence of the media. He asked where was *CNN, CBS, ABC, NBC, New York Times, Washington Post, USA Today* and *Fox*? *BET* gave the conference a mention when it interviewed Alexis Herman. The only Black newspaper that did extensive coverage was *The Final Call*, which featured a special pull-out section.

The signal sent by the summit coverage was that, even though Dr. Sullivan and President Rawlings were able to pull together 14 heads of state of African countries, along with vice presidents and foreign ministers from the Diaspora, it was not deemed newsworthy that these leaders from Africa demonstrated that they had a concern about relationships with Africans in the Diaspora, in particular those from North America.

At the conference were such people as Reverend Mrs. Jesse Jackson, Andrew Young, Kweisi Mfume, Dr. Robert Franklin, Alexis Herman, Carl Ware (president of the African side of Coca Cola), David O'Reily from Chevron Corporation, Minister Louis Farrakhan's wife Khadijah Farrakhan and his chief of staff Leonard Muhammad, Reverend Willie Wilson of Washington, D.C., Dr. Leonard Jeffries of

AFRICA AND THE WORLD: REVISITED

New York, Susan Taylor, Coretta Scott King, Dr. Dorothy Height, Dick Gregory, Mayor Wellington Webb from Denver, Colorado, and many, many more who came together with these African heads of state. Is this not newsworthy?

There was not thorough coverage of the fact that the conference focused on things of interest to Africans in the Diaspora, such as dual citizenship, a pet project of President Rawlings who is looking for the best way to implement dual citizenship in Ghana for Africans in the Diaspora. There were workshops on agriculture, business, trade, investments, democracy, education, health, as well as special forums on women and youth. All of these things took place at the summit.

Jules Wijdendasch from Suriname, South America attended. The attendees from African countries included Robert Mugabe from Zimbabwe, Abdou Diouf from Senegal, His Excellency General Mathiwu Kerekou from Benin, General Gnassingbe Eyadema from Togo, Benjamin Mkapa from Tanzania, Vice President of Kenya, His Excellency Ketumile Masire of Botswana, King Mswati from Swaziland, King Letsie from Lesotho, a large delegation from Nigeria, Henri Konan Bedie from Cote d'Ivoire, Ahmad Kabe from Sierra Leone, and Omar al-Bashir from the Sudan. Is this not news?

The speech of President Rawlings was delivered on May 19th, the 75th birthday of Malcolm X. In his speech, he mentioned this and also showed how Malcolm worked to make the connection between Africans in the Diaspora and those at home in Africa. He talked about Marcus Garvey's influence on Ghana's first president Dr. Kwame Nkrumah, the black star in the Ghanaian flag and the idea of a unified Africa. He also talked about the fact that Dr. Martin Luther King Jr. came to Ghana on the Independence Day of Ghana on March 6, 1957 and was inspired by what he saw before returning home to continue his struggle in America.

This was a great conference and it was the kind of positive movement on the African continent that should have received wide coverage by the Western press, which finds everything negative to say about Africa. It reminds one of what was said in a memo by National Security Advisor Zbigniew Brzezinski to former President Jimmy Carter about keeping African Americans away from making a meaningful connection with Africa and African leaders.

So, we salute Dr. Sullivan and those who took time out of their busy schedules to attend and report about this great summit. Dr. Sullivan said, as he arrived in Ghana, "Less talk and more work. I did not come to Africa to make a good speech. I came to do some serious work."

To this end, Dr. Sullivan launched the People Investment Fund for Africa (PIFA), designed to change the future of young small-scale entrepreneurs on the continent. He opened the way where all of us who are concerned for the development of Africa and our place in that development can invest in this fund. Where was the media coverage of this very powerful and important summit?

29

African Bloodletting:

The Betrayal of Africans in the Diaspora

Looking at a picture of an African woman with both her hands cut off on the cover of the *New York Times* makes a person who loves Africa and African people leery. The madness of conflict in Sierra Leone as seen in the press leaves one to wonder how people of the same nation could commit such atrocities against one another.

I once read, "The first victim of war is always the truth." Television reports have highlighted the first so-called high-tech war in the Horn of Africa between Ethiopia and Eritrea. Other African countries suffer the same scourge. The killings in Algeria continue; some are saying that the government is killing its people and blaming it on Islamic terrorists, while the government is saying Islamic terrorists are killing innocent women and children in order to overthrow the government.

The conflict in Guinea-Bissau has produced thousands of refugees fleeing to nearby countries. The fighting in the Democratic Republic of the Congo (formerly Zaire) has southern and central Africa in turmoil. America's former ally, Jonas Savimbi of UNITA in Angola behaved like a spoiled brat during the peace process, took his marbles, went home and picked up his gun. Now, thousands are dying. More are starving and being displaced from their homes.

AKBAR MUHAMMAD

In Uganda, President Yoweri Museveni has his share of problems in the North with the Lord's Resistance Army, a Christian fundamentalist group trying to overthrow the government in the name of the Lord. The rebels, who recently bombed Kampala, are now fighting in the West. Museveni is sending troops into the Democratic Republic of the Congo to support the overthrow of his friend whom he helped into power. It is obvious that Museveni, as a military man, did not read about the dangers of fighting a war on three fronts.

There is a war in the Sudan – a war that America and England could end tomorrow by no longer supplying John Garang through their surrogates. They could force him to the peace table overnight by simply drying up his aid as they have done in Angola and Mozambique.

Somalia is another example. Its leadership cannot seem to form a unified government, one that could address the needs of the people. Tremendous suffering and killing still continue.

All of these things are happening in Africa while Africans in the Diaspora are looking to Africa with so much hope and promise. Africans across America and the world are talking of investment, tourism, teaching, living and working in Africa. It is so unbelievable that, after 400 years of robbery by Europeans, Americans and others, Africa is still rich in human and natural resources. Her people, who have gone through all of this, are still warm, beautiful and full of hope.

Very rarely does the Western press publish stories or photographs of the many positive events that take place on the continent of Africa. Instead, the press shows only bloodletting and corruption. It is almost as if they are saying, "If you had any hope, plans or intentions for Africa, forget it!" The bloodletting is a betrayal of all those who have positive plans for Mother Africa.

Africans in the Diaspora must pool their resources to spread positive messages about Africa and help resolve disputes on the continent. Dr. Leon Sullivan, chairman of the African/African American Summit, is having his fifth summit in Accra, Ghana on May 15-22, 1999. The tentative program is good; however, in light of what is happening on the continent, I would humbly and strongly suggest a *conflict resolution* forum. So far, Dr. Sullivan is blessed with commitments from 15 African heads of state who plan to join him at this historic conference. I hope Dr. Sullivan can bring these heads of state together with the best minds of Africans in the Diaspora in this vital council. All of them love Africa and want to see an end to the bloodletting and suffering.

Many African leaders may not see Africans in the Diaspora helping in this arena because they cannot see the root or understand the depths of the problems in Africa. However, I must quote a Turkish proverb that I learned on one of my many trips to Turkey: "The eye sees everything but itself." Africans in the Diaspora have never had an opportunity to have a meaningful role in helping Africa. It may be surprising to see what positive input this overlooked group could have in solving some of the problems on the African continent. The people on this tremendous continent have nothing to lose and everything to gain.

AKBAR MUHAMMAD

30

ALI, JUST SAY NO!

A few days before Christmas, the news circulated concerning Muhammad Ali being recruited by a group called Hollywood 9/11. The group was encouraged by the United States government to use its skills and abilities to help America in its so-called war against terrorism.

It was reported by the press and circulated throughout other media that Muhammad Ali would make a propaganda clip to be shown directly to the Arab and Muslim world. The information about the clip was quite straightforward; it was designed to encourage the outside world, and the Muslim world in particular, to see America's point of view.

One problem for Ali, the Black American community and especially the many millions of Black Americans who are Muslims is that we do not know the next move of the Bush Administration in their war against terrorism. Another problem is that neither the Black American community nor its leadership has been involved in the foreign policy of the United States government. We only react to the policy set by the government. We have no voice in making or determining foreign policy or its direction. I think that it is criminal to use Muhammad Ali in this way.

Ali, as a Muslim, is loved not only by Muslims in America, but he is loved and respected by more than 1.5 billion Muslims around the world. The words of the scriptwriters and translators of the script into the languages spoken by Muslims around the world may represent a gamble for Ali. He has to understand that the scriptwriters are the same ones in the recent past who have vilified Arabs and Muslims in films that were presented to the American public. Their mindset is not to protect the image of Ali or Islam, but to promote the image of America.

If this war should continue and the American people become dissatisfied with the war as they did with the Vietnam conflict, then potentially this poses a conflict for Ali as a champion in the Black community and as one of the Muslim's heroes. Though his mind is clear, Ali's battle with Parkinson's disease makes it difficult for him to articulate what he wants to say. A consultant for the Hollywood 9/11 group stated that Ali's presence would not relieve them of having to tread carefully.

Mr. Hossein Ziai, director of Iranian Studies at the University of California in Los Angeles, stated, "If it is something that, let us say, comes out as if he either insensitive or co-opted, that could lead to some sort of a negative impact." Doing an ad for Coke, as Ali has done previously, is different from doing an ad for an ongoing war in the Muslim world, where thousands of innocent men, women and children may be killed and written off as collateral damage.

Jack Valenti, president of the Motion Picture Association of America, one of the members of Hollywood 9/11, considered a Muhammad Ali ad to be one of several options to promote the image that America freely accepts Islam and the Muslim way of life. They would like to position him as a spokesman for Muslims in America. The problem with this is that Ali has never claimed to be a spokesman for Muslims in America.

Also, many Muslims may have different opinions about their religious freedom to practice Islam in America other than that which Hollywood 9/11 would like to project to the rest of the world, especially in light of thousands of Muslims being imprisoned, cut off from their families, and denied the right to an attorney because of their names and religion. Recently, one of President George Bush's secret service agents with an Arabic name became a victim of racial profiling and was ejected from a commercial airline just before takeoff.

One of the reasons that Ali should *just say no* is because Muslim charities have been attacked and their accounts frozen. The many poor Muslims who have benefited from these charities do not see the charities as supporting terrorism, but as supporting the needy. This, again, produces a problem for America's credibility among Muslims all over the world. Muhammad Ali has to take all of this into consideration before he gives his consent to do a public relations piece for Hollywood 9/11.

Ali, just say no. There are other opportunities for you to help. Let it be on your terms, not something designed by Hollywood.

I have watched the ability of Hollywood to build and dismantle leaders. They have the ability to influence people who are not familiar with certain periods of history, causing the viewer to accept the image projected on the screen.

In the movie, "Ali," Will Smith did an excellent job in his role as Muhammad Ali. However, the portrayals of President Mobutu of Zaire and the Honorable Elijah Muhammad were terrible. Mobutu was projected as a thin, frail and feeble old man, but at the time he was not. The Honorable Elijah Muhammad was given a foreign accent instead of a Georgia accent, which was his birthplace. The whole projection of the Honorable Elijah Muhammad vis-à-vis Ali was a distortion of the leader of the Nation of Islam. If they could find someone such as Marvin Gaye's daughter, who looks so much like Khalilah, Ali's second wife, then surely they could have found men who looked more like the Honorable Elijah Muhammad and Mobutu.

My appeal is that Muhammad Ali should *just say no*. He should wait, be patient and see how things unfold before making this kind of commitment to

Hollywood 9/11. There are a lot of famous athletes in America who are known throughout the world; however, this famous athlete is Muslim. In the movie "Ali," when Will Smith walked out of the courtroom and stated a litany of reasons why he should not fight for America in the conflict in Vietnam, the entire audience broke out in applause. He was talking about the plight and struggle of Black Americans at that time, and even today.

Since September 11, 2001, the plight, struggle, suffering and pain of African American communities have been pushed off the front burner. If Ali says no to Hollywood 9/11, then he should say yes to fighting for prison reform; yes to liberating the nearly two million Black men and women in prisons across America; yes to the battle against the menace of crack cocaine; yes to working to see that young brilliant Black American students can get into college and graduate; and yes to doing something about the dilemma of single parent homes. Black women are now being pushed off welfare and forced to provide for their children and themselves. Ali, say yes to wanting to fight to get Mumia Abu Jamal off death row; and to Jamil Al-Amin (H. Rap Brown), another brother who has a long history in the struggle, receiving justice in his case.

I want to see Brother Mumia liberated. I'd like to see Ali become a champion for reparations across America. Ali can use his tremendous connections to open business opportunities in Africa and the Caribbean. He can also use his connections and image in the fight against AIDS in America and Africa. There is much that Muhammad Ali can do to make an impact on the struggling Black masses in America and Black people throughout the world, without allowing Hollywood 9/11 to package him for Bush's war on terrorism.

Ali, *just say no.*

31

ISRAEL'S DIRTY WORK IN AFRICA

The recently published book, "Gideon's Spies," by Gordon Thomas is quite revealing. The book is selling at a rapid pace, not only in America, but throughout the world. If it continues to sell, it will overwhelmingly top Victor Trotsky's book, "By Way of Deception." The indigenous Africans and Africans in the Diaspora who can remember the book, "CIA's Dirty Work in Africa," need to look into the section of Thomas' book titled, "An African Connection." It shows the role that Mossad played in destabilizing many of the liberation movements in Africa and causing entities to divide against each other, changing sides as they saw necessary. They would find it most interesting.

Thomas describes in vivid details Israel's double-dealing in Africa. Some critics saw it as only Mossad, and not the government and people of Israel. But can one say that the CIA is not the United States government? The term that Mossad uses for them (by the former Israeli Prime Minister David Ben-Gurion in 1951) is "Ha Mossad le Teum," meaning, "The Institute for Coordination."

AKBAR MUHAMMAD

What is most interesting in the book is Israel's work with the South Africans during the apartheid era in allowing them to work in Dimona, where Israel produces nuclear bombs at its nuclear plant. While America is battling with Pakistan, India, North Korea and China over their nuclear capabilities, nothing is said about Israel. The Israelis are the ones who are training the South Africans. They assist the South Africans in setting off nuclear explosions in the southern part of the Indian Ocean and they continuously work to undermine liberation struggles throughout the African continent.

Thomas tells of the cases of killing people who Israel perceives to be enemies of the state. The manner in which Israel commits these crimes could only be described as state-sponsored terrorism. How hypocritical it is for America to single out nations as sponsors of state terrorism when America's number one ally in the Middle East – Israel – has a history of nearly 50 years of state-sponsored terrorism. According to Thomas, these singled-out nations could not hold a candle to what Mossad has done.

If one wanted to get an insight into Israel's dirty dealing, double dealing, double crossing, murdering, bombing and creation of mayhem, they should read this book. One of the most interesting and compelling parts that Thomas reveals is what the Israelis or Mossad calls LAP, which stands for the Department of Psychological Warfare. This department is responsible for hiding the truth of events by twisting news headlines to make the public think another reality is the truth.

Many may remember Robert Maxwell, the British media tycoon who was involved in the Iran arms sale. Most of us who read about it had no idea of the involvement of Oliver North and others of his kind. Maxwell and Mossad schemed to sell American arms through Israel to the Iranians, where billions of dollars were made, while Iran was described in the media as an enemy. They were giving arms to one side in order to help the Iranians kill their Muslim brothers in Iraq. At the root of this was the LAP.

AFRICA AND THE WORLD: REVISITED

In the 13th chapter of "The African Connection," Thomas mentions that Mossad orchestrated the uprising that led to Kwame Nkrumah's overthrow because of his relationship with China and the direction he was taking Ghana.

Also in that chapter, he mentions the Congo and Mossad's work with the Bureau of State Security (BOSS) in South Africa, stating that BOSS matched Mossad in blackmail, sabotage, forgery, kidnapping, prison interrogation, psychological warfare and assassination. Like Mossad, BOSS had a free hand in how it dealt with its opponents. The two services became bedfellows, often operating in tandem. They moved through Africa enjoined by a secret understanding between Israel's Prime Minister Golda Meir and the Pretoria regime.

Thomas goes on to say the first big deal or results of this relationship had been to export uranium to Dimona. The shipments were carried on commercial flights from Johannesburg to Tel Aviv, listed on the manifest as agricultural machinery. South African scientists traveled to Dimona and were the only outsiders who knew the true purpose of the facilities.

When South Africa tested a crude nuclear device on a remote island in the Indian Ocean, an Israeli scientist was present to monitor the blast. In 1972, the heads of state for Israel and South Africa ratified an understanding: If either country were attacked and required military assistance, the other would come to its aid. Israel supplied South Africa with substantial quantities of U.S. manufactured arms and, in return, was granted permission to test their first nuclear device, which was produced in Dimona.

It was, again, Mossad that introduced BOSS in South Africa to the new methods that they were using on Palestinians in the Lebanese interrogations, such as sleep deprivation, forcing a suspect to stand at a wall for long periods, squeezing genitals and a variety of other mental tortures, ranging from threats to mocked execution.

Mossad teams traveled with BOSS units within neighboring Black countries on sabotage missions. They showed the South Africans how to kill without leaving any embarrassing evidence. When Mossad offered to locate African National Congress leaders living in exile in Britain and Europe for BOSS to kill, the bureau welcomed the idea. The South African government finally vetoed the proposal, fearing that they would lose the support they had among die-hard conservative politicians in London and other places.

Again, according to Thomas in his book, the work of Mossad and the South African Security Service was the driving force behind the CIA's dirty work in Africa. I would recommend that the crop of African leaders called the "new leaders of Africa" should absolutely make "Gideon's Spies required reading.

32

ZIMBABWE: TAKING BACK LAND FROM WHITES MAY BE CONTAGIOUS

There have been overt press attacks on President Robert Mugabe of Zimbabwe for the last few years. The attacks have been vicious, imbalanced and unwarranted. Reading these reports, one would say that the attacks were because President Mugabe is resisting democratic change and unjustifiably wants to take land from Whites.

The antagonists should be brought forward and asked the following questions: Are you trying to justify that the White people are entitled to the land which their fore-parents robbed from the indigenous African people in Zimbabwe? What about the people who were forcibly removed from their land? What about those freedom fighters who sacrificed, fought and lost their lives for the independence of Zimbabwe? Are these people not justified in having some of the land that was stolen from them during the colonial period? Are you saying that we should forget that?

I think the words of Mugabe during the height of these vicious attacks against him and his government should be recalled. He stated, "England and the Western world feel that what I'm doing is unjustified and that the White landowners should be compensated." He suggested, "Then, let England compensate them for the land that I want to give back to my people."

AKBAR MUHAMMAD

The West and some African governments are fighting against this so hard because they know it could have a ripple effect. This could inspire other landless Africans. Taking back land from Whites may be contagious.

At this period in our history, the subject of reparations is on the hearts and minds of millions of Africans, on the continent and throughout the Diaspora. The question of reparations at the United Nations Conference on Racism in Durban was blocked by the United States, which tried to marginalize the whole issue. Reparations is not only for the descendants of the horrors of the Trans-Atlantic Slave Trade, but reparations and compensation are issues for those on the African continent who were fleeced, robbed and abused by the Western world.

Why would the House of Representatives join the Senate in the last few weeks to talk about imposing sanctions on the country of Zimbabwe? They want to impose the kind of sanctions they did in Liberia. The plan is to increase dissatisfaction among the members of the President's cabinet. They are hoping that the curtailment of travel outside of their country will cause the people of Zimbabwe to turn against their leader. The governments of the Western world are specialists at dividing people against their leadership, in hopes that those same people will oust their leaders from office either through voting or fighting to overthrow them.

In the last Organization of African Unity conference before the emergence of the African Union, the Honorable Minister Louis Farrakhan and I had the opportunity to sit and talk with President Mugabe on two occasions. If one could have listened to Mugabe's reasoning, without the poison of the Western press, then one would come away with a totally different perception.

An example of this poison is the accusation that President Mugabe is older now and just trying to hold on to power at an old age. An enlightened view would be to compare him to Robin Hood. He is in the waning years of his life and he has looked over his shoulder. He wants to give something substantial to his people.

AFRICA AND THE WORLD: REVISITED

He tried to be balanced and civil when independence came to Zimbabwe. He realized that there were certain things that White farmers were doing that the country needed for the sake of its economy. Therefore, he was reasonable enough to leave them intact and allow them to function in a country where they previously had oppressed and misused Black people as well as robbed them of their land. He was willing to forgive and even forget if they would help the economy of Zimbabwe move forward. Hindsight is 20/20.

Hypothetically, if President Mugabe had told White people to be prepared, for in the near future the land that they had robbed from the African people must be returned, would it have been less painful? The feeling is that Whites have helped the country in their own way, but they have really helped themselves without helping the masses of African people.

Those who understand the political and historical dynamics on the African continent perceive the vicious attacks on President Mugabe by the Western press as an attempt to render him unsuccessful before the same mood arises in other countries, such as Namibia, Botswana, Kenya and Zambia. In South Africa, where Whites from the repressive apartheid regime still own land and businesses, they have retained a privileged status for themselves while still oppressing many of the Blacks.

The real objective of this vicious media campaign throughout the world, depicting the supporters of President Mugabe as thugs, is designed to stop him so that the confiscation of the land robbed from the Africans will not spread to other parts of Africa.

AKBAR MUHAMMAD

33
Show "Touched By An Angel" To Highlight Sudanese Slave Controversy

When a story appeared in the September 20, 1999 edition of *USA Today* stating that the September 27th season premiere of "Touched by An Angel" would dramatize the issue of slavery in the Sudan, my first thought was that the war against the spread and influence of Islam among African Americans had escalated.

There is no doubt that the Sudanese slavery controversy has touched all Americans. I have followed this controversy since 1992 and have made numerous trips to the Sudan. The issue of slavery in Africa and the world is of most interest to African Americans because we were the last group to experience the enormity of slavery here in America.

When the Sudanese slavery controversy first broke, there were two countries involved – Mauritania and the Sudan. The issue was first promoted by the American Anti-Slavery Group, a Jewish organization headed by Dr. Charles Jacobs. When Dr. Jacobs, who is White and Jewish, saw that the anti-slavery program had limits because of his involvement, a Black group, financed by an unknown entity, emerged to form the Coalition Against Slavery. Its focal points were Mauritania and the Sudan; Mauritania was soon dropped and attention shifted to the Sudan.

The group advanced the idea that Arab Muslims were enslaving Black Christians in the Sudan, and this image was being presented to Americans. Yet, this was the farthest thing from the truth.

Minister Louis Farrakhan weighed in on this issue in a meeting with John Garang, leader of the Sudanese People's Liberation Army. They met for hours. In that conversation, Garang never mentioned the issue of slavery in southern Sudan. He only spoke of justice for his people and the suffering of the people in the south.

Countless meetings with Sudanese President Omar al-Bashir, Dr. Hassan al-Turabi of the Popular Congress Party, and other Muslims from Khartoum have the Sudan estranged from them because of allegations that Sudanese officials were enslaving Black Christians. President Bashir stated that, as with other African countries, there are conflicting tribes in the Sudan that quarrel, kidnap people and trade them for weapons or food.

There is a problem in Uganda with the Lord's Resistance Army, a Christian fundamentalist group seeking to take over the Ugandan government. This army raids villages, holds captives, forces captives to work and even makes them join the army. Yet, the term "slavery" is not used. They are called "captives of war" but you have not heard one person saying this is a form of slavery.

Why haven't Congressman Donald Payne and writers at the *Baltimore Sun* who have visited the Sudan, met with President Bashir and addressed the accusations of slavery?

This opening episode of "Touched by An Angel" in my opinion is another attack on the tremendous influence that Islam is having throughout the Black community, in the Western Hemisphere and especially among African American men. What the show will try to convey to believers in Islam is, "How can you love a religion that supports the enslavement of Black Christians who only want their freedom?"

AFRICA AND THE WORLD: REVISITED

There are many church ministers and congressmen joining this bandwagon. This issue can be settled overnight if Americans would stop making surrogate countries such as Uganda, Kenya, Eritrea and Ethiopia part of the conflict in the Sudan. These are nations that America armed, claiming they needed protection from the Sudan. However, America's arming of Ethiopia and Eritrea led to war between the two countries, leaving thousands of Africans killed. It was all an elaborate attempt to topple the government of the Sudan.

If government-run slavery exists in the Sudan, then we too condemn it. But if this show is propaganda to divide the Black community and attack those sympathetic to Islam, then we denounce its writers and the continuous attempts to give Africa and Islam a bad image.

Former President Jimmy Carter has visited the Sudan many times in an attempt to bring about peace. Ask him about slavery in the Sudan. President Bashir was asked about slavery last May at the African/African American Summit Conference in Ghana. What was his answer and why wasn't it reported in the Western press?

Last year, the *New York Times* reported slavery in Brazil. Why hasn't there been controversy surrounding Brazil? There, farmers use Indians and Blacks to work on their fields under the threat of death. There are reports of indentured servant slavery in villages in West Africa. Why hasn't controversy surfaced around that? In India, there are reports of children in bondage working in servile conditions. Why haven't you heard of this? I will tell you why.

There is focus on the Sudan because the current Sudanese government is a fiercely independent government that America has bombed and falsely accused of terrorism. This television show is the West's last ditch effort to discredit Islam and the Sudan. Christian Broadcasting Network's attempts, with Pat Robertson, to influence Black ministers to speak out against dubious claims of enslavement of Black Christians have failed.

AKBAR MUHAMMAD

So, during the epoch of Minister Farrakhan's sabbatical, they want to launch a show using notables like Della Reese to convey a false idea. I am sure Ms. Reese doesn't know of the chicanery used in this episode. My only hope is that those who watch this program will question and discern whether there is an ulterior objective there.

34

The Sudan and Slavery Issue

The unnecessary attacks on the Sudan continues. After returning from Africa, I tuned into the Christian Broadcasting Network with Pat Robertson. They were showing a story about slavery in the Sudan. As I watched the suffering of the Sudanese people, I wondered why America would continue to support John Garang, leader of the southern Sudanese, knowing that the more support they give him, the greater the pain and suffering will be for the Sudanese people.

The suffering and so-called persecution of Christians in Khartoum is being blamed on what is wrongly described as a militant, fundamentalist Islamic regime that has declared a holy war on the Christians in the south. If we want this to stop, America has to withdraw its support of Garang through its surrogates. America has to tell Israel to stop supporting him and using the bases of Kenya and Uganda. This war and suffering could stop overnight if America and others weren't so bent on distorting the image of Islam and continuing the campaign through their support of Garang.

Around the world where there have been civil wars, it often results in the warring factions being forced to a peace table. Bosnia is an example. We have also seen this happen in Africa. We saw America force Jonas Savimbi to the peace table in Angola. We saw America force the Renomo rebels in Mozambique to a peace table. We saw them force the Ethiopians and Eritreans to a peace table.

AKBAR MUHAMMAD

Yet, the suffering continues for the people of southern Sudan. At the root of their suffering is not the struggle of John Garang for independence or just and fair treatment for his people, but the propaganda machine of the Western world and an attack of the government of Khartoum (Sudan). Will the two sides of this "instigated" civil war be forced to a peace table?

I am surprised at the position taken by Reverend Jeremiah Wright, a progressive Christian minister in Chicago, Illinois, for whom I have great love and respect. I am surprised that he has become a victim of this propaganda. The eyes of those who have joined in the fray against the government of the Sudan should have been opened when America bombed a pharmaceutical plant under the pretext that the plant was producing biological weapons of warfare for terrorists. This attack was not questioned because of the propaganda against the Sudan even after it was proven that President Bill Clinton had made a mistake.

I have been to the Sudan on many occasions and I have been to the southern region. I have talked to the people in the south. I have met with Garang on three different occasions. I arranged a meeting for Minister Farrakhan with Garang to discuss his problems as it relates to the Sudan being used for an all-out attack on Islam. The claim is that the Sudanese government is "enslaving" its people.

There is a war going on and, in war, there are people who are captured. Did they consider the situation that recently broke out in Bosnia with the Christian Serbs and Muslims as slavery? People were held, families captured, men tortured and women raped and killed. More than 60,000 women were raped because they had Islamic names.

I think that if there is a coalition of Christian ministers who are concerned that slavery is an issue in the Sudan, they should go to the Sudan and talk to the government officials and Garang. I have not heard him speak about slavery in all of my conversations with him; I have only heard that from others.

AFRICA AND THE WORLD: REVISITED

We must consider the events occurring in Uganda where the Lord's Resistance Army is fighting a war against the government of Uganda. They capture people. They hold them. Is it talked about as Christians "enslaving" people? No, they are called hostages and captives of war. When it comes to an Islamic government however, this same practice is referred to as slavery. The organizers of the propaganda plot know very well the bitter feelings and emotions that arise when slavery is mentioned among Black Americans.

I would hope that Christian ministers and Americans, in general, would wake up and not allow the propaganda machine of the American government to use their voices to say that these Muslims have declared "jihad" and are enslaving Black Christians.

When I read Reverend Wright's reflections for the New Year, I have to ask about the story that he told of how a man sold all of his cattle and money to redeem his family. He walked to the north for many days to find his family. He paid an Arab to help him find his children. When he confronted the owner to purchase their freedom, he was able to negotiate the release of his wife and five-year-old, but their master would not relinquish the nine-year-old. Now, if you are talking about slavery, why did not the so-called Arab master who had captured the man's wife and children just take the man as a slave if slavery is indeed going on? Why would the man find an Arab to negotiate? The picture is not clear. It leaves much to be desired.

I believe that Reverend Pat Robertson's method of using the guise of giving food and aid to actually distribute Bibles that are used to preach against the government in the north is not proper. He further exacerbates the situation.

AKBAR MUHAMMAD

35

AMERICA'S FAILED POLICY IN THE SUDAN

The United States of America has to take the full responsibility for the ongoing conflict in the Sudan. The main group fighting against the government of Khartoum is supported and supplied by America. The propaganda machine of the Western press has made this appear as a religious war, which is the farthest thing from the truth. Informed people know much better.

The American people have not been clearly informed about the bombing of a pharmaceutical plant in Khartoum after the tragic destruction of the two American embassies in Kenya and Tanzania. The bombing was portrayed as hitting a plant that Osama bin Laden used to make chemicals for chemical warfare. Later, it was found to be just a pharmaceutical plant as the people of the Sudan previously stated. Consequently, the owner of the plant is now suing the American government for damages. This is just one tragic example of the failed policies of the American government in the Sudan.

Another failed policy is that the United States is the cause of the ongoing war in the Sudan. John Garang, leader of the Sudan People's Liberation Army (SPLA), held out from the peace process only because America has been supplying him with weapons, money and support. The press made it appear that the government of Khartoum is stopping relief supplies from going to the despondent women, children and elderly of southern Sudan in an attempt to make the people in that area suffer. This is not true.

America knows that it has been using Kenya and Uganda in the relief efforts to supply arms and other needed equipment for Garang and the SPLA to continue the war against Khartoum. Also, they bring out his wounded soldiers and aid the movement of his troops under the cover of supplying humanitarian aid to the southern Sudanese.

The media propaganda war about slavery is just about over. The real issue now is the oil in the Sudan. Now it has become an economic war, and why the people are still fighting is not clear. The best peace plan thus far is the Libya-Egypt one. I would hope that the United States of America is not so blind by its dislike of Libya that it is opposing this plan.

The National Democratic Alliance, which was a group of those struggling against the government in Khartoum, has written various news releases that Garang is out of control. The need to sit at the table and resolve this issue is long overdue. Sadiq al-Mahdi, leader of the Umma Party and former head of state of the Sudan, has gone back to Khartoum.

The tragedy of the Eritrean-Ethiopian War that has caused the loss of nearly 70,000 lives was rooted in America arming both countries. America's reason for this was that it needed to help them protect themselves against the Sudanese.

Now that Eritrea has suffered in this war, it is no longer a base for the Sudanese opposition. It is time to end this long tragic war for the people of the Sudan. America could end this war tomorrow by forcing Garang to a peace table or cut his supplies. They can

do the same to bring him to the peace table as they did in Angola and Mozambique.

American policy should be aimed at stopping the death and suffering of an entire nation of people, and not "balkanizing" Africa. A United States of Africa will solve 75 percent of Africa's problems.

36

ONE MORE BIG LIE: AMERICA ACCUSES LIBYA OF SLAVERY

The American government, United Nations and other Western nations have caused the people of Libya untold suffering with inhumane sanctions and bombings. Now, the American Anti-Slavery Group headed by Dr. Charles Jacobs, a Jewish consultant, has accused the Libyan government of selling Black people. In part two of a three-part article written by Dr. Samuel Cotton in the February 8-14 editions of the *City Sun* newspaper in New York, he states that in Libya, Black people are being sold into slavery. This was a step further than he had gone in part one, where he said that the president of Africa's largest country, the Sudan, had six to eight slaves in his home at Khartoum.

An invitation has been extended to members of the Black press, including Mr. Cotton and his publisher, to visit the Sudan. To date, neither of them have responded. Mr. Cotton's quotes and most of the information called "research" were obtained directly from the American Anti-Slavery Group based in Washington, D.C. via Dr. Jacobs, who has been using the pain of a Black Mauritanian to justify his attack on the religion of Islam.

AKBAR MUHAMMAD

It is well known that Blacks in Mauritania suffer under racism and mistreatment by the country's rulers. He is using this suffering to judge a religion and not the people of that religion. It is also an attempt to divide an already divided Black community on the issue of Islam and the influence of the Nation of Islam under the leadership of Minister Louis Farrakhan.

The cartoon used in part three shows an Arab slave master beating a group of Black men and women. Dr. Jacobs has sent a press release to 95 percent of the African American newspapers across the country. He is using the old FBI trick of planting stories (misinformation).

The Libyan people have a history of being wrongfully accused and later vindicated. They are still suffering from unjust sanctions imposed in April 1992. The vindications have not been correctly presented to the public by those who are responsible for the sanctions. So, in the eyes of the public, the Libyans are still suspects.

Anyone who has read Muammar Qadhafi's "Green Book" can attest to the fact of how Qadhafi feels about Black people and their eventual ascension to a position of power in the world. He and the people of Libya have opened their doors to Black people from around the world and have struggled to show a true sense of brotherhood for Africans at home and in the Diaspora.

As in all other cases, I am sure that this big lie being circulated by the American Anti-Slavery Group against Libya and the Sudan will eventually be exposed as another manipulative device. I believe their propaganda is intended to propagate division among Black and Arab people both in America and Africa.

AT THE HEART OF AFRICA

VII
ECONOMICS & DEVELOPMENT: BUILDING BLOCKS OF FREEDOM

Nelson Mandela and Muammar Quadaffi in Libya

AKBAR MUHAMMAD

Robert Williams, Zaki Bruti, Muammar Quadaffi, Preston Wilcox, Dr. Khalid Muhammad, Dr. Musa Hawamda

37
Planning For The Future?
Consider Africa

Recently, President Jerry Rawlings of Ghana addressed the National Black Master of Business Administration Association's convention that took place in Detroit, Michigan. The overall convention was attended by more than 10,000 people. The spirit of the event was heightened by young Black businessmen and businesswomen working in corporate America or their own private businesses as they plan for the future. It was an ideal environment for networking. Speakers, such as George Fraser, lifted the desire and inspired everyone in the audience to strive and plan well for the future. During the conference, former U.S. Ambassador Andrew Young spoke on the topic, "International Business Opportunities for the Young Black Entrepreneur." The focal point of international business in his forum was Africa. He indicated that, even though there are problems, there are also tremendous opportunities in Africa. He expounded on some of the opportunities, mentioning that it is imperative that the African American community become involved.

He spoke the morning before President Rawlings delivered his keynote address. If you listen to both of them, it would appear that they had exchanged notes and conferred with each other before they spoke. However, I personally know that they did not because, after Andrew Young's speech, he rode with us to the Detroit airport to receive President Rawlings.

AKBAR MUHAMMAD

The keynote address delivered by President Rawlings, attended by more than 3,000 participants, brought the weeklong conference to a rousing close. There were many thought-provoking points made in his address. Many of those who attended the conference expressed a desire for his speech to be printed as a booklet and distributed throughout the African American business community in America.

One of the points that he made that captured the audience was the invitation extended to them to convene their conference in the year 2000 on the African continent. He emphasized that they represent a symbolic "Joseph-type" (from the Bible and Holy Qur'an). Joseph was sold into bondage, went down into Egypt, received the learning and knowledge of the Egyptians and, after much suffering (going to prison, etc.), had a conscious, spiritual awakening. He remembered he was a descendant of Africa. He remembered his family. And when famine plagued the land, he had the key to the granary.

President Rawlings was blessed to use effective words with the young, brilliant brothers and sisters. He showed them that, even though they had been away from home and suffered in a strange land, this was not a totally negative experience. The great knowledge that they had acquired allowed them to be able to now "come back home" and use this knowledge to push Africa ahead, as we go into the next century.

As a resident of Ghana and a friend of the people and leadership of Ghana, I will ask the Minister of Communications to, by all means, put President Rawlings' excellent speech on the official website of the country of Ghana as well as publish it in a booklet so it can be circulated to Africans in the Diaspora.

38

Liberia Can Be Rebuilt

I have just returned from my fourth trip to the naturally rich land of Liberia. Not only did I find this West African country rich in natural resources that include minerals, timber, farmland and waterways, I also found that the country is rich in human resources. You still find a willing group of brothers and sisters ready to learn, work and rebuild their country.

Liberia held out hope 153 years ago for Africans in the Diaspora who saw no hope in staying in America or the Caribbean. In the early 1800s, when White Americans began to see the problems of the Africans in America, action was taken. A group of prominent Americans came together to explore the idea of providing a colonial retreat for the so-called freed people of color. This retreat would begin on American or African soil. Central America was even considered at one point.

In December 1816, a group of Americans formed the Society for the Colonization of Free People of Color of America. This organization later grew into the American Colonization Society. By 1820, the first group of ex-slaves was on its way to settle in Monrovia (named for President James Monroe). One African in the Diaspora considered a founding father of the early repatriation movement was Edward Wilmot Blyden.

AKBAR MUHAMMAD

By 1847, Liberia was a Negro Republic on the West Coast of Africa. During the period when the Honorable Marcus Garvey was building his movement, he believed that Liberia should be the mecca for the African race. Although Garvey never set foot on the African continent, his vision was that Liberia should become the headquarters for his United Negro Improvement Association (UNIA).

Now more than ever, Liberia needs the sons and daughters of Africa to help in her rebuilding process after seven years of a most destructive civil war. The relationship of the Liberian government and its people cannot and must not be based on the prevailing view of the Clinton administration and his African advisors. The people of Liberia have suffered enough. If Western and Eastern donor nations, International Monetary Fund, World Bank and African Development Bank are slow in stepping in to aid Liberia, then we must, as a world community, do our part. We must also put pressure on all representatives in Washington, D.C. to do more toward this effort.

My eldest daughter Samimah Aziz, a Howard University graduate, recently visited Liberia. As a result of her experience, she is now promoting a "People to People for Africa" campaign to make the public aware of rebuilding efforts and the need for aid and assistance in Liberia.

In June, a delegation of government ministers headed by Liberia's First Lady Jewel Howard Taylor will visit seven U.S. cities. The purpose of the visit is to inform American communities of the current social and political events in Liberia. Delegates will also provide information about investment opportunities in Liberia and encourage African Americans to consider Africa as a place to earn money and use their expertise to aid in the development process.

… AFRICA AND THE WORLD: REVISITED

39

BLACK FARMERS FOR AFRICA

Recently, Dr. Ridgely Muhammad participated in a trade delegation to the West African country of Liberia. The trade delegation was organized for business people and potential investors to see what is happening politically and economically in Liberia and determine how African Americans can assist in the rebuilding process.

Dr. Ridgely is the managing director of the Nation of Islam's 1,600-acre farm in Georgia. He earned a doctorate degree in Agricultural Economics from Michigan State in East Lansing, Michigan. I invited Dr. Ridgely to join the delegation because he is committed to helping and supporting the thousands of Black farmers across America who are now in a battle with the U.S. Department of Agriculture.

Our farmers are men and women who grew up on farms and studied and earned degrees in Agriculture. They love the earth and are experts in their trade, but they have not been afforded an opportunity (in the past 15 years) to use their knowledge and skills to make a decent living in America.

AKBAR MUHAMMAD

It only makes sense that Black farmers begin to look toward Africa for answers. Africa is abundantly rich with fertile land, but the land is under-utilized and in need of the skills and expertise of the Black farmer. My vision is to see our farmers working and training young people in Africa. Many displaced African farmers have gone into the capital cities of their countries, looking for work and placing a burden on the infrastructure. With a training program in place, these displaced farmers can go back to the countryside to earn a living with pride and contribute to feeding their nation.

Liberia, in particular, has a need for the expertise of trained farmers. During the seven years of conflict, many young Liberians left the land to engage in fighting or flee from the fighting. Those who left the farms were not encouraged to maintain their skills nor did they have an opportunity to learn from their elders the traditional techniques used in farming. Liberia needs those who can help her farmers see the value of the land and teach them to produce enough food to feed the nation and beyond. The agricultural community needs the technology of canning and food processing. These are some of the areas to be developed in Liberia as she rebuilds.

It is important to remember that Liberia has not received the foreign aid that was promised to her after the conflict ended. I articulated to government officials and President Robert Taylor that the concerned world community would not agree with the type of politics that allows Liberians to continue to suffer as they have during the past 10 years, especially when the politics are centered on potential donors' likes or dislikes of Liberia's leadership.

In spite of the delay in foreign aid, Liberians are willing to move ahead. Some of the potential donor nations, civic organizations and other business entities that can help Liberia use the "corruption in Africa" as a poor excuse for not giving aid. They say they are afraid of corruption. I ask, what about the more than $17 billion that America sank into Russia? This investment in Russia came from the government and private sector in America, most of which was lost to corruption. Today, Russia is one of the most corrupt nations you can find. Criminals are not only in the streets, but they can be found among government officials, from top to bottom. When it comes to investing in Africa, funding and pockets are closed, with poor excuses.

There are millions of Black people who have not considered Africa as a serious place to invest, train and do humanitarian work. We must begin to change our thinking. We are the sons and daughters of Africa. If we do not seek and take advantage of the opportunities in Africa, someone else will. Liberia is ready to receive us!

The Minister of Agriculture in Liberia will be on tour in America with the First Lady of Liberia Jewel Howard Taylor in June 2000. He and the other ministers with him will be best able to articulate about farming in Liberia.

AKBAR MUHAMMAD

40

Bush Dismisses Black America as He Targets West African Oil

Historically, slaves were considered "black gold." However, in modern times, the new black gold is oil. Not just any oil, but the oil from the soil and shores of Africa. The Bush Administration has "aimed their guns" at Africa and begun firing. Many articles featured in international magazines and the *New York Times* have mentioned West Africa as an area chosen for strong consideration for America's oil supply.

The Bush Administration's focus on African oil may even extend beyond West Africa. They are looking for oil from Angola to Guinea Bissau, from Libya, Chad and the Sudan to the Central African Republic. The opening shots were fired when Secretary of State Colin Powell made a visit to Angola and Gabon.

The first volley took place when Jonas Savimbi, leader of the UNITA movement, was killed in Angola in a so-called firefight. He had become useless to America and the West. I believe he was killed when he became a headache. His position did not fit into the new American plans for oil from West Africa. Thereafter, Secretary Powell arrived in Angola to confer with the leaders of the Angolan government. Ironically, they are not having oil talks with the leaders of Angola after years of America's support to UNITA, which was a reactionary movement trying to replace the government of Angola.

From Angola, Secretary Powell traveled up the coast to Gabon, which is an oil-rich country with a lot of land and only 1.2 million people. Omar Bongo, a Muslim, is the leader of this predominately Christian nation.

You do not have to be an expert or specialist in international affairs to know that, if President George Bush turns a deaf ear on sound advice and goes ahead with his plans to attack Iraq and unseat Saddam Hussein, this will interfere with the oil flow from the Middle East. This administration fumbled the ball in Venezuela, which happened to be an important oil supplier to the United States in the Western Hemisphere. When the Bush Administration secretly supported a coup against Hugo Chavez, the legitimate president, they saw that his removal could cause a bloody civil war. The instability created by a civil war would have meant no oil at all for America. Venezuela is still the third largest supplier of oil for the United States. As a result, they are now focusing on West Africa as the source of the new black gold.

Africa has a population of nearly 800 million people, and Muslims make up half of this population. Had the Bush Administration considered the repercussions of its ill-conceived plans to attack Iraq, they would have addressed the fact that some of the key countries that the United States is trying to cultivate for oil supplies are predominately Muslim or nations that are led by Muslim leaders. A war could cause a need to replace the oil supply that would have come from the Middle East. America would have to target the Sudan, Chad, Libya, Nigeria, Angola and Gabon, and on a smaller scale the country of Guinea Bissau in West Africa, to replace the supply from countries such as Saudi Arabia, the United Arab Emirates, Kuwait and Iraq.

Slaves from West Africa were considered black gold 200 years ago not only needed for their physical labor, but there was a critical need for slaves to turn the wheels of the American economy. Today, there is a need for this new black gold, this oil, to turn the wheels of the American economy and the entire Western world. The question is, "Where is the African American community on this proposition?" We have a historical right to be involved. America deals with Africa without any thought of our inclusion. We have knowledgeable people among us to deal with these oil concerns. They would welcome the opportunity to make money in the oil business and they should be invited.

There are not just millions, but billions of dollars made every day in the oil industry. Very few African Americans are involved in this business. As America focuses its guns on West Africa as a new source of oil, let us not stand on the sidelines or be marginalized in this situation.

Bush plans to go to Africa in the year 2003. He is sending a message that this is the White boy's business and the nearly 40 million descendants of Africa will be locked out. The signal sent will be that African Americans have no place in the oil business, or we have not been considered. Bush dismisses Black America in his quest for West African oil.

AKBAR MUHAMMAD

Akbar Muhammad, President Mugabe of Zimbabwe

41
STOLEN LAND, WHITE OCCUPATION

The question of land, its occupants and who should be its proper owner have been raised in Zimbabwe. The root of the controversy is that President Robert Mugabe and his government are determined to give land back to the people from which it was stolen when European conquerors first arrived in the country. Because President Mugabe is determined to right a historical wrong, he has been called everything from a Hitler, dictator and power monger who wants to stay in power, to an abuser of human rights. All these names are coming from the Western press. Members of his party, who are fighting for the rights of those who fought a long, bitter struggle for the independence of Zimbabwe, have been called thugs.

To add insult to injury, U.S. Secretary of State Colin Powell used his platform when he spoke to the press to criticize President Mugabe for reclaiming the land taken from his people when the Whites came to Zimbabwe and drove the Zimbabwean people off the land. Europeans put the indigenous population of Zimbabwe in a condition that was virtually tantamount to slavery. Now that the pendulum of justice is beginning to swing in the opposite direction, there is an outcry against the Zimbabwean people who want the land that was taken from them returned.

Secretary Powell, a descendant of the horrible Trans-Atlantic Slave Trade, could have taken this opportunity as a Black man to show that he is sensitive to this problem. He could have told his bosses in Washington, D.C. that, before he makes a statement condemning President Mugabe and his government in Zimbabwe, he wanted to gain an informed opinion about his view, and then issue a statement.

However, showing that he is still a good soldier, he articulated the position of his bosses in Washington without getting his brother's view or position.

During the Organization of African Unity (OAU)Summit in Lusaka, Zambia, Minister Louis Farrakhan had a private meeting and an opportunity to listen carefully to President Mugabe and his position in regards to why it is necessary to reclaim the land stolen from his people. Since the Europeans supported the theft of African land and continue to support those Europeans who live on stolen land, it should be England and other European nations who compensate them. European nations stood by, watched and benefitted from this theft. Therefore, they should step up to the plate and compensate the Zimbabwean people. They should not be compensated from the struggling economy of Zimbabwe. The reason why Europeans want to draw the line in Zimbabwe is that what is happening in Zimbabwe is contagious. It will spread to southern Africa just as AIDS is spreading through southern Africa today.

In South Africa, Black people were promised housing and land five years ago, but the promise was not kept. And so we saw last week, the masses have taken it upon themselves to occupy the land by force. The same fear is running in Botswana where there are tremendous amounts of land that are owned and occupied by Europeans. The same fear is also in Namibia, Zambia and Kenya. These countries fear thatwhat was started by Mugabe in Zimbabwe will spread and Black people as far away as East Africa will begin to demand that White people return stolen land to the indigenous people.

This is why the statement of Muammar Qadhafi at the OAU Summit in Lusaka was met with applause when he said that the land of Africa belongs to the Blacks. To back up his statement, after the conference ended he flew to Zimbabwe to support Mugabe and his people in the struggle to regain their land.

AFRICA AND THE WORLD: REVISITED

AKBAR MUHAMMAD

42

AFRICA AND THE EFFECTS OF EURO-TOURISM

There are few countries on the African continent that do not want to enjoy the benefits of a strong movement of tourists. Tourism produces jobs and brings in hard currency. This includes everything from landing fees for major European countries to more cultural items, i.e. wood carvings, clothing, restaurants, cultural sites and historical landmarks. Most Africans who travel to the continent from the Diaspora are in search of a cultural experience. However, there is a level of tourism that has affected the moral fiber of Africa. In my travels to 31 of Africa's 52 nations, I have seen the negative effects of Euro-American tourism and its influence on a budding society that would like to use its country's beauty and people to bring in capital.

I have seen countries that allow European women to lie around the poolside on the beaches half-nude or completely nude. I have witnessed European women who travel in search of Black gigolos and European men who come looking for little boys or girls to satisfy their sick, perverted sexual appetites. I have seen the dangers of the American or European tourist lifestyle, the growth of prostitution, the movement of drugs and the influence of cigarettes on a traditionally non-smoking society. I have traveled to countries that were typically non-drinking countries due to their religious and cultural backgrounds, but have now flooded their market with alcohol to satisfy the tourist trade.

The influence of the Western film industry throughout Africa via music, videos, satellite and cable programs provides outlets for tourists as well as exposes the negative influences of sex and violence on a people not accustomed to such perversions. These films give the local people a view that the people of the West are exactly like what is shown in its films. This form of cultural imperialism has affected the family structure to the extent that Africans are adopting a more Western attitude in their styles and manners, and are rejecting their own. Pornography films have found their way into the country as well, to satisfy the appetites of tourists with sexual programs with local prostitutes. Prostitution has been legalized in many places.

African society must not stand by and use the weak excuse that prostitution is "the oldest profession" in the world while their young girls and boys are abused in the name of the tourist industry. Some of the same controls that were used in the days of military governments may not be updated in this ever-popular movement of democracy. However, this type of negative cultural imperialism, under the guise of tourism, is going to destroy the flowers of African society – our youth.

VIII
WAR & CONFLICT: THE MORAL ACCOUNTABILITY OF HIDDEN IMPERIALIST HANDS

AKBAR MUHAMMAD

Minister Louis Farrakhan, Mustapha Farrakhan, Pres. Jerry Rawlings, Akbar Muhammad, Captain Kojo Chikata in Ghana

43

AMERICAN PRESIDENT'S HYPOCRISY TOWARD AFRICA

President-elect George W. Bush, Secretary of State Colin Powell and National Security Advisor Condoleezza Rice must scrutinize the hypocrisy of President Bill Clinton's policy in Africa. Long before *The Economist* magazine published the story about America's support of Uganda and Rwanda against the Democratic Republic of the Congo (DRC), the hypocritical tactics of the U.S. were well known by most Africa-watchers.

How could America prosecute a case against Charles Taylor, based on what they describe as "blood" diamonds, and then engage in the support of those forces in the Congo that have caused death and destruction, disease and division? The Congo is as large as the entire western half of the United States. U.S. Under-Secretary of African Affairs Susan Rice described the conflict in the Great Lakes area of Africa as Africa's first world war.

The problem is that America has weighed in on the side of the forces that are at the root of the conflict, mainly Uganda and Rwanda. The death and destruction in the Congo now affects nine nations. Because of America's support and supplies to their two allies, Uganda and Rwanda, she has caused the suffering that has taken place in that area. If America withdraws her support, it would help bring Rwanda and Uganda to a peace table sooner and perhaps diffuse the rebel forces fighting against the legitimate government in Kinshasa.

AKBAR MUHAMMAD

During President Clinton's historical 12-day visit to Africa at his meeting in Rwanda, he apologized for America not acting in a timely manner to save the lives of almost one million people during the Rwandan genocide. We would hope that the new American administration will not fail to learn the lessons of history and repeat the tragedy that the Clinton Administration promoted in Africa.

Will America stand by again as resources are utilized to cause the death of another million people in the Congo? Instead of Secretary Powell talking tough about what he will do to Iraq, he needs to talk about cleaning up the mess that America made in the Great Lakes area of Africa.

If Africans could take American leaders to an international court and charge them for their meddling in this region, then America and Europe could be sued for the death and destruction of the people in the Congo. America would have to pay a price, not only for their involvement on the wrong side of this issue; we have to also take into consideration that it would rekindle awareness of the facts about America's involvement in the killing of Patrice Lumumba.

The legacy of American support for a dictator (Joseph Mobutu) during the Cold War would also surface. Mobutu was a leader who abused the resources of his country and sank it into ruin before he was overthrown. These facts would all come to light. The American government's support of Mobutu, as we look back in history, was wrong. President-elect Bush and his advisors on Africa have their work cut out for them.

The press in Europe and America have not put one word in their papers about the initiatives from Libya to help resolve the conflict in this area. Muammar Qadhafi has spent time and money trying to broker a peace deal. He has been successful in talking to the leaders. He has been able to call them all to Libya to face one another to see how they can best resolve this issue. No mention of this was made in *The Economist* magazine or the Western press.

AFRICA AND THE WORLD: REVISITED

The American public should want to know why America has put herself in the middle of this conflict. What is the strategic interest of the United States? These are the questions that the new administration will have to answer on its policy toward Africa.

AKBAR MUHAMMAD

44

War in Africa:

The Root of Conflict Between Eritrea and Ethiopia

Recently, the world woke up to hear the news of the ongoing conflict between Eritrea and Ethiopia – a dispute over their shared border. This may be a half-truth regarding a hidden agenda instigated by the U.S. and Israel disguised in the form of aid.

Secretary of State Madeleine Albright, during her visits to Africa over the last two years to countries surrounding the Sudan, promised aid and assistance. During the same period, Israel set up relations with Eritrea, selling them weapons and using the Sudan as the reason that Eritrea had to be armed against a so-called "fundamentalist state." This opened a way for the Sudanese opposition to establish a base in Eritrea.

America, Israel and, perhaps, others have cultivated relationships to aid and help the new country of Eritrea. Some of the same military aid was given to the Ethiopians. When aid is needed to feed the masses of people and provide better health facilities and education, these well-wishing donors cannot be found. Instead, much of their aid comes in the form of military hardware. With both Eritrea and Ethiopia armed by America and Israel, the two African countries turned on each other, using their weapons to fight each other instead of against the so-called enemy, the Sudan.

At the root of the conflict in Africa are foreigners – America and Israel. The latest word is that this may evolve into a hi-tech war – the first of its kind in Africa, according to reports from the British Broadcasting Corporation (*BBC*). A hi-tech war? Who sold Africans hi-tech equipment, and for what reason? Now, the United Nations is pleading, "No more sales of arms to either side." What hypocrites!

If only the leadership of Ethiopia and Eritrea would hear concerned Africans in the Diaspora lifting their voices to speak against the enemies of Africa. These enemies of Africa are making a fortune by selling weapons of mass destruction to poor African nations to get them to use these weapons against one another.

As a result, innocent lives are being destroyed and governments are being disrupted. They are spending money to engage in conflicts and war instead of developing the African people. This must cease in order for Africa to move forward.

45

President Charles Taylor and the Liberian People

Most Americans and the world witnessed a few months back the arrest of four so-called members of the news media in Liberia. The picture was painted to the world that this oppressive dictatorial government arrested four newsmen, held them captive and, only after international pressure, released them. The four men stated that all they wanted to do was film what was going on in Liberia. This is the farthest thing from the truth.

As the truth begins to unfold, we see the hand of America and England directly involved in trying to paint an ugly picture of the Liberian leadership and what is taking place in the country. They are doing this once again, in order to justify the imposition of sanctions on this West African nation, which is struggling for balance after a seven-year devastating civil war. If the American and British media would have told the whole story, people would have seen the plan that was about to be perpetuated against President Charles Taylor and the people of Liberia. Time and space will not allow us to give the full details but, with enough being said, I will try to make it simple.

One of the four journalists, Timothy Lambon, who was born in Zimbabwe when it was called Rhodesia, now claims to have dual citizenship with Britain and South Africa. He was found to be a helper of Ian Smith, who had fought against Robert Mugabe's liberation forces and was known to torture and kill many freedom fighters. In 1980, after the freedom fighters succeeded in liberating Zimbabwe from South Africa, he then moved to South Africa. While living there, Smith worked with the apartheid regime, doing the same work he had done in Zimbabwe, torturing and killing those struggling against the oppressive apartheid regime.

In Liberia, a script upon which they were to base their report was found in the hotel room of the four journalists. This script said such ridiculous things about Charles Taylor; that he had a fleet of Rolls Royces; he wanted to be the godfather of West Africa; he earned upwards of $300 million a year in diamonds, etc. The story was distorted at best; however, if they could have gotten footage and interviews to make the story believable, this would have been played in America and England. This film would have set the stage for people to condemn the leadership of Liberia and its people, as well as impose unjust sanctions.

There are several examples of unjust sanctions being placed on other countries. This scenario has been demonstrated before with the Sudan. Unjust sanctions have been imposed on the Sudan because America favored John Garang – not because they loved him, but because he held a key to the newly found oil fields of the Sudan. Therefore, the Sudanese government had to be condemned as an oppressive, extremist, Islamic government that was killing and enslaving poor Christians in the south.

Another example is Libya being accused of the Pan Am bombing and the subsequent sanctions imposed on the country. This caused the Libyan people to suffer and lose more than $30 billion during the period of these sanctions. Now that the trial is unraveling and it looks as though Libya will be exonerated, this appears to have been another attempt to create an atmosphere to justify the sanctions, as well as give the government of America an excuse to carry out their war against fundamentalist Islam.

Now, we are hearing talk of sanctions against Zimbabwe. This same kind of propaganda is being used today against Liberia and Zimbabwe. Therefore, the whole story must be told in order for Africans in the Diaspora to recognize the design and scheme against African leaders and governments that do not "play ball" with the West or refuse to become "boys" for America, England and other nations in Europe.

AKBAR MUHAMMAD

46

Why Liberia?
Why President Charles Taylor?

Is President Charles Taylor the first victim of regime change on the African continent at the hands of Western nations? It is clear that Westerners do not want any African leader in power who will interfere with their long-term goals and plans for Africa.

We all thought that the first victim of regime change under the Bush Administration would be President Robert Mugabe of Zimbabwe. But it is obvious that the Bush regime has run into some problems trying to remove Mugabe from his legitimate position as the elected president of Zimbabwe as quickly as they would have liked. America, under the Bush Administration, tried to put the icing on the cake by issuing an executive order for sanctions against 72 members of Mugabe's government and also other sanctions that included prohibitions of Americans spending U.S. currency in Zimbabwe.

The media coverage throughout the world reported that President Taylor has been indicted on war crimes charged by a United Nations-sponsored court. What a United Nations-sponsored court is, remains to be seen. After the Iraq War, the United Nations, which has virtually lost all of its credibility, is now turning to Africa to try to flex its muscles by issuing an indictment against President Taylor in conjunction with the courts of Sierra Leone.

Sierra Leone is a country that is struggling for its own balance. How does this indictment help stabilize Africa? The other issue that we must look at carefully is that President Taylor was in the country of Ghana pursuing a peace accord with the rebels against whom he is fighting in his country. This current fighting has caused tremendous suffering for the people of Liberia. President Taylor left his country to meet with those whom he thought could bring an end to the fighting.

At the same time, the indictment is issued and Ghana is pushed to arrest President Taylor, which would create additional chaos and confusion in West Africa. President John A. Kufuor of Ghana showed great strength in not playing into the hands of those who wanted President Taylor arrested. To get another African government, Ghana in this instance, to execute on the arrest while the man is pursuing a course of peace, should be totally unacceptable to African leadership.

The hypocrisy of what is happening to President Taylor is that America and Europe preach democracy and democratic reform around the world. If governments, such as England, France and America, do not like the election results after African leaders, under very trying circumstances, move toward a democratic process and elect a president, they (England, France and America) push to create chaos and confusion in those countries. Through the chaos and confusion, they attempt to remove or overthrow the legitimately elected president.

I wish that space and time would allow those of us who have visited Liberia, the refugee camps in Cote d'Ivoire and Ghana to describe the hardship, struggle and tragedy of those camps. These governments are struggling to run the camps with a small amount of UN aid. When we witness people who are suffering, then we will understand the importance of peace and stability in the West African region. This latest attack on President Taylor and the threat of his arrest only serve to further escalate the crisis.

AFRICA AND THE WORLD: REVISITED

This is the importance of strengthening the African Union. President Olusegun Obasanjo of Nigeria and President Thabo Mbeki of South Africa were in Ghana trying to help negotiate for peace. I wonder what their reaction was when they heard that there was a warrant for the arrest of President Taylor and the host government of Ghana was being pushed to execute the arrest. When news of the indictment hit the media, David Crane, an American and former U.S. Defense Department official, was quoted as the person answering all the questions and pushing for President Taylor's arrest. Crane is the prosecutor for the special court of Sierra Leone. He was deeply involved in the pursuit of Taylor's arrest.

In these times, we wonder why Liberia and Charles Taylor. Liberia is a country that is rich, rich, rich. It has abundant oil reserves off its coast. It is rich in gold, diamonds, timber and iron ore. It also has rubber tree plantations. It is obvious that the long-term plans for this part of Africa does not include leadership such as that of President Taylor. If he was being arrested for his support of the Revolutionary United Front (RUF) in Sierra Leone, what would prevent the next step being the indictment and subsequent arrest of the leader of the Libyan Revolution, Muammar Qadhafi and President Blaise Compaore of Burkina Faso?

The grounds for their arrests would be their support of President Taylor during the days of Liberia's civil war when he was struggling against the forces of former President Samuel Doe. We must remember that America backed, paid and protected Doe. America set up one of their main CIA offices for sub-Saharan Africa in Liberia. When the CIA saw that Doe was on the ropes, they abandoned him and allowed him to be killed in a very vicious manner.

Before you begin to charge President Taylor, you must look at the historical background. This is why in Africa, the African Union and its strength is important. Western nations (The G8) have been working hard to weaken the African Union and thwart its movement by instituting the campaign to fund the New Economic Partnership for Africa's Development (NEPAD).

In President Taylor's case, one can compare it to the days of slavery in America. When the slave master caught a slave running away, starting a rebellion or just doing something that the master disapproved, he would beat or maim the slave in public in order to instill fear in the other slaves. The removal of President Taylor as the legitimate president of Liberia is the same case. Instill fear in the other African leaders by demonstrating to them that this is what we will do to you if you get out of line with us.

In this instance again, President Mugabe of Zimbabwe is a prime example. He is an African leader who had the audacity to reclaim stolen land from White settlers. For this policy, the Western world wanted to make an example out of him by instituting sanctions to warn other African leaders not to try this.

These two presidents have been charged with similar human rights violations. As far as Taylor's guilt in these charges, we have to say to the Americans and Europeans, "He who is without human rights violations, let him cast the first stone."

47

THE QUESTION OF SLAVERY IN AFRICA

Recent news reports by journalists in the Western media and throughout the world have intensified their focus on the ongoing problem of so-called slavery in Africa. The latest news reported was about a slave ship leaving the country of Benin and sailing along the west coast of Africa. In the final analysis, it was discovered that it was not 250 children on board but a shipload of 40 children. *Time* magazine did a double-fold spread on this drama. Quite naturally, as news like this is read in the press and seen on television, it brings great pain to Africans in the Diaspora. For descendants of the barbaric Trans-Atlantic Slave Trade, it is doubly painful.

There are ongoing news reports of slavery in the Sudan, alleging that Muslim Arab militants backed by the government of the Sudan are enslaving Black Christians and Animists in the southern region of the country. In the last few years, the Animists have been added to the equation. When the stories first emerged, they said Muslims were enslaving Christians. However, when the realization surfaced that there were more Animists than Christians in southern Sudan, the Animists were added to the news stories. Animists, being of the African traditionalist faith, are also pitted against Christians. Publicly redeeming or buying Black slaves from so-called Arab slave traders is something we must look at carefully and not be swayed in our rush to judgment.

AKBAR MUHAMMAD

Before Reverend Al Sharpton left for his trip to the Sudan, Minister Louis Farrakhan asked me to say two things in consulting with Reverend Sharpton. Minister Farrakhan gave me the following verse from the Holy Qur'an: "When an unrighteous man brings you news, look carefully into it – lest you harm a people in error and be sorry for what you have done." In addition, he said, "When you go into a man's house, try to go into the front door and not the back door."

Unfortunately, circumstances did not permit me to give these words to Reverend Sharpton. However, I must give credit to him on his trip to the Sudan. Although he did go in through the back door, crossing the border from Kenya into the Sudanese Peoples Liberation Army (SPLA) controlled area, he would not allow himself to be engaged in the so-called public act of buying slaves back. This is a big fraud perpetuated by entities that seek to pit Christians against Muslims. By exploiting a war and its prisoners, they are attempting to hurt the harmonious relationship that Muslims and Christians share in many parts of the world.

All one has to do is to consider this point: If the slave traders are holding 100 slaves in the SPLA regions, asking for money to free them, why do not the armed SPLA fighters (who are in control) just shoot the so-called slave traders and liberate their people?

The Sudan is a long and complex history of British rule, the style of which has consistently been one of divide and conquer. Northern Sudan was cut off from southern Sudan, and functioned much like apartheid. When the British freed the Sudan from their rule, instead of annexing the Sudan onto Uganda, they joined southern Sudan with northern Sudan. This exemplifies how the map of Africa was configured - it was drawn so that there would always be ongoing conflicts.

AFRICA AND THE WORLD: REVISITED

The Sudan, the largest country in Africa, is a bridge country. It touches eight other African countries. With its newly found, tremendous oil fields, as well as its large gold reserves, it has become the prize of the Western world for economic reasons. This is why certain entities in Europe and America want to exercise control over the Sudan.

I have written on this issue many times. And I have stated again and again that the 15-year civil war and suffering in the Sudan would cease overnight if America, Europe and Israel would stop giving weapons and equipment to John Garang, SPLA rebel leader. This would force him to the peace table.

The countries that they have used as surrogates to pass war supplies and weapons to the SPLA are countries that are suffering right now because of this. One can ascertain why God has not blessed these countries in recent years, especially since they have allowed themselves to be used in a war that has taken more than two million lives and caused untold suffering. These countries are Eritrea, Uganda, Kenya and Ethiopia.

We should not and cannot allow people with different agendas to use the Black community in America to fuel their agenda, namely the American Anti-Slavery Group and Christian Solidarity International. The American Anti-Slavery Group, headed by Dr. Charles Jacobs, has an agenda with its continuous attack on the Sudan. Doesn't it seem logical that, if he is running an anti-slavery group, then he should be concerned with slavery all over the world, not just in the Sudan? In addition, the Christian Solidarity International has a negative agenda. Their agenda is to attack Islam on the African continent because they feel that Islam is in competition to Christianity.

AKBAR MUHAMMAD

Michael Jackson recently announced that he will travel to the Sudan to free some enslaved children. This will become a celebrity media show where well-known celebrities come to give money for a picture showing them freeing a slave. If they feel that they want to help the Sudan, they should go in through the front door – Khartoum. They should get both sides of the story before they make statements referring to the government of the Sudan as backing and sanctioning the enslavement of Black Christians and Animists.

There is a war going on in the Sudan and, in wartime, prisoners are captured, as in the Vietnam War. Prisoners are traded for goods needed on one side or the other. I have not heard or read in one Western newspaper that the Lord's Resistance Army, a fundamentalist Christian group fighting in Uganda, is enslaving child soldiers or individuals from villages in their struggle to make Uganda a fundamentalist Christian state. They use the term "kidnapping" to describe how young men are taken and forced to fight, but they don't call them slaves. I do not believe that a parent in West Africa or anywhere in Africa is knowingly selling their children into slavery for $15.

There is a new book written by a Jewish South African, entitled "Islam's Black Slaves," which adds more fuel to this fire about Islam condoning slavery. We should know the difference between commercial human bondage and servitude slavery, which has existed in the world. Commercial human bondage was started with the Trans-Atlantic Slave Trade. It was the most barbaric and inhumane method of handling human beings that the world has ever seen. If one wants to read about the history of slavery in the world, the book "Slavery: A World History" by Milton Meltzer begins the history of slavery in ancient times with the Greeks and Romans. Most of their slavery came about through wars. But there is no comparison anywhere in the history of slavery as in the Trans-Atlantic Slave Trade.

I recently spoke to a Black female producer of a major news program. This young lady said she disagreed with one of the things she heard from members of the Nation of Islam about a conspiracy in the newsroom. She said it doesn't have to be a conspiracy, that those behind the news stories are mainly White men with the same mindset. They project images that would make you think they communicate or talked to each other, but the fact is that they all think alike.

AKBAR MUHAMMAD

48

WHY A STRIKE ON IRAQ JUST BEFORE RELIGIOUS HOLIDAYS?

A world gone mad. A president who obviously is not focused and cannot make decisions that reflect sound judgment. Bad advice and bad judgment are blinding President Bill Clinton. His blindness is now clearly visible with his call for strikes on Baghdad and the Iraqi people nine days before the Christian holiday and three days before the Muslim world begins its holy fast of Ramadan.

Mr. President, your blindness has caused many countries to turn against America, as evidenced by the demonstrations and protests in capitals around the world. A country as great as America should never be seen as a bully, bombing a nation that cannot defend itself and killing innocent men, women and children.

The two largest religious communities in the world begin their holiday seasons with the specter of America and its only follower, Britain, bombing and killing.

The Christian world would much rather sing about peace and goodwill toward mankind, shop, give gifts, listen to holiday cards, visit with family and friends, and celebrate the birth of the Prophet of Peace, Jesus Christ. Muslims would love to start their holy fast of Ramadan, not eating and drinking from sun up to sundown, in peace and wishing peace to all. This is the time of year for reflection, prayer and asking God for guidance and forgiveness for our shortcomings and sins.

Yet, during these holy days and sacred times of the year, we have been forced to listen to the news of destruction and death for the people of Iraq. We have also been forced to take sides on the impeachment issue and moral questions surrounding our president.

Why would you, President Clinton, turn the majority of nearly 1.4 billion Muslims around the world against America and your administration? If the masses of American people were told the truth, and then were asked whether you should bomb Iraq at this time, they would say, "No, we have had enough. We have had to deal with Ms. Lewinsky and you, Mr. President. You need not live out the movie, 'Wag The Dog,' about a war being started to take the attention off a president who gets involved in an act that would discredit him and his office."

The sober and fair-minded would say, "Let the Muslim world enjoy its holiday, the fast of Ramadan, and let the Christian world enjoy its holiday and New Year season."

Mr. President, you have made enough enemies inside this country. Now, your blindness has caused you to increase your enemies outside America, as your trip to Palestine/Israel was a failure.

Members of the press are saying that you discussed your intentions to bomb Iraq with Israeli soldiers. The American people are pouring more than $10 billion in aid to Israel every year in the form of loans, gifts, military aid, etc. If one-third of that amount was spent on the problems of the Black community, we could redirect millions of lives, increase employment and decrease the growing prison population that is now out of control. The untimely bombing of Iraq is like an arrow that has left the bow – you cannot call it back.

The writers of history will say that President William Jefferson Clinton flew to Palestine/Israel in December 1998 to save a failed peace accord that he initiated, returned to America in the middle of an impeachment hearing, and made a decision to bomb Iraq. He failed to save the peace accord and he failed to eliminate Saddam Hussein, the leader of the Iraqi people.

One can hypothesize that the author of the book, "The Tragedy of Lyndon Johnson," will have an opportunity to write about a real tragedy: The Tragedy of William Jefferson Clinton.

AKBAR MUHAMMAD

49

Nelson Mandela on President Bush: "No Foresight – He Can't Think Properly"

The strong words of former South African President Nelson Mandela at the International Women's Forum held in Johannesburg in January 2003 may reflect the thinking of many African leaders. Some would like to say even more about their disagreement with President George Bush. They may even tie it to the cancellation of his trip to five African nations in early January 2003. He used the weak excuse that the cancellation was due to the current crisis in Iraq. Yet, during his recent trip to Europe, he stated that terrorists or others would not deter him from making trips to other parts of the world to attend conferences. Many Africans have watched the United States focus on West African oil and the administration attempt to buy African leaders to keep them quiet, as the United States pursues this unjust war in the Middle East.

If and when this war starts, it will undoubtedly kill innocent men, women and children. Africa has a population of nearly 800 million, half of which are Muslims. There is no doubt that the Muslim population of Africa from north to south will feel a sense of pain to see the death and destruction of their brothers and sisters in Iraq. Mandela is calling President Bush someone who is pushing America to the brink of war, and describes him as a person who has "no foresight and cannot think properly." These are strong words from the former president of South Africa, who went on further to state that, "Mr. Bush's warmongering is for the control of Iraq's oil."

AKBAR MUHAMMAD

Those who thought the freedom fighter Mandela, who was incarcerated in South Africa thanks to the assistance of the CIA, had lost any of his fire, should listen to his next statement. He stated, "Mr. Bush is disregarding the United Nations because the secretary general, Kofi Annan, is a Black man. The position that America is taking against the United Nations would have never happened if the secretary general were a White man." He makes a strong point because, in the last few months, we have barely heard a word from Secretary Annan in the American press. It is almost as if he has been marginalized and stripped of his power. It is well known that he disagrees with the way that America is pursuing this attack on Iraq.

Mandela did not stop there. He ratcheted up his attack to a new level on America's misguided foreign policy as it pertains to Iraq. He criticized the United States for complaining about Iraq's human rights record, asserting that America's conscience is far from clean. Mandela pointed out the atomic bombing of the Japanese cities of Hiroshima and Nagasaki during World War II, asking the question: since they decided to kill innocent people in Japan, who are still suffering from that bombing, are they now pretending they are the policeman of the world?

He gave great joy to those of us who follow African news, to see how the Pan African Congress of South Africa cheered Mandela for his strong stand. We feel that Brother Mandela's stand will give strength to other African leaders who are not bought and paid for by the West with a little aid. They should speak up strongly and clearly.

In February 2003, South Africa plans a big anti-war march and it will be a source of inspiration across the African continent for demonstrations against this unjust war. As the African Union begins to prepare for their meeting in July in Mozambique, there will be no doubt that one of the agenda items will be the African Union's stand against the war in Iraq.

AFRICA AND THE WORLD: REVISITED

Nelson Mandela, at 84 years old, still has the clarity of mind as well as his fire. He cannot be bought or sold, so therefore he speaks as a free man and a free African who is speaking out not only for African people, but also against injustice anywhere in the world. I send a warm African salute to a genuine African hero, Brother Nelson Mandela.

AKBAR MUHAMMAD

IX
POLITICS & GOOD GOVERNANCE:
UNDERSTANDING TRUE MODELS OF LEADERSHIP

50

Target Jesse Jackson:

The Dismantling of a Black Leader

In the book, "Shakedown: Exposing The Real Jesse Jackson" written by Kenneth R. Timberman, Reverend Jesse Jackson is presented as not having one bone of honesty and never performing a single, sincere act for the millions of Black people who see him as a Black leader. This book is not only an insult to Reverend Jackson, in light of his many years of work and sacrifice, but it is an insult to the Black community which he has affected.

Reverend Jackson did not approach the Black community saying, "Look, I am an angel and God has placed a halo around my head." He came to the community as a fallible human being, trying to do what he thought best to make a difference for people. We all have our frailties, shortcomings and weaknesses. We believe that Allah (God) can use our strengths – for example, the ability to think on our feet. One must possess the ability to recognize the traps, plots and plans of those who are against Black people receiving justice in a historically unjust society.

AKBAR MUHAMMAD

I strongly reject, detest and abhor the accusations in Timberman's book. Regency Press, the publisher of the book, must have an agenda for the 2004 elections by publishing such trash. I feel this is part of the smear campaign targeted at Reverend Jackson's domestic life. This attack commenced soon after he stated that he found discrepancies in the past presidential election and fought to have a recount. When they write the history of this period, they will say that he had a major impact on the voting habits of Black people in this country – the likes of which we had not seen since Jimmy Carter's election in 1976.

Even those who dislike him will admit that he is the impetus behind many Black people going to the polls. Many Blacks in the past did not concern themselves with voting in local, gubernatorial, congressional or presidential elections. However, he persuaded them to go to the polls. Minister Farrakhan registered to vote for the first time in his life because of Reverend Jackson's cogent reasoning. This caused thousands of Muslims, who previously disregarded the electoral process, to register.

After reading the book, one might conclude that Reverend Jackson is a communist or communist sympathizer, by the way that Timberman positioned Jack Odell with him. By making inappropriate references, he distorted Reverend Jackson's trip to South Africa. He states that America had to maintain a relationship with South Africa because of the Soviet Union, which was seeking to control the entire southern area of the African continent.

This is similar to former President Ronald Reagan's justification of his support of the late Jonas Savimbi. The South African government, Israelis, British and Americans supported Savimbi's fight against the legitimate government of Angola and keep that fight going, which took the lives of nearly a million people. Angola has more landmines than any other country in the world. Most of these landmines were made in the U.S. Today, we hear about the children in Sierra Leone whose limbs they accuse the Revolutionary United Front (RUF) of chopping off. They accuse RUF members of this atrocity, yet how often have we read that American-made landmines have maimed thousands of young soldiers, children and elderly in the country of Angola? The U.S. backed all of this.

For Timberman to imply that Reverend Jackson had another motive for visiting South Africa is absurd. He states that America was trying to justify maintaining her relationship with South Africa. He criticized Reverend Jackson as though he was doing something against America by going there to rally the people, though the people rejected Reverend Jackson.

Timberman closes a chapter by saying that he did not get his mansion. He stated that Reverend Jackson was trying to buy a small house outside Chicago on a lake, which belonged to the Kellogg family for $295,000. Reverend Jackson was attacked, and Timberman states, "Jackson didn't get his mansion, perhaps in part of the vigilance of a *CBS* news reporter, but he learned to identify a new enemy, the Jews." This description of that event is inappropriate. The modest house that Reverend Jackson has on Constance Street and the cars that he drives do not match up to the picture painted of him. Timberman talks about the source of revenue for Jackson's few suits and about his friends who help pay some of his expenses.

He discusses how Reverend Jackson asked President Bill Clinton to pardon prisoners who had worked on behalf of the cause of justice for the Black community and may be innocent of trumped up charges levied to discredit them. However, Timberman makes it appear that Reverend Jackson wants to free hardened criminals who are menaces to society. He needs to read the scripture in the Bible that says, "Proclaim freedom for the captives." Again, this is a terrible way to describe a man who, after 45 years in the struggle, is left without any credibility or right to stand before Black people for whom he has sacrificed his time, family, wealth and health. Let us all in one voice say, "Shame on you, Kenneth R. Timberman."

As I went through the book, I unsuccessfully searched to find passages where Timberman gave Reverend Jackson credit for some accomplishments. I can verify that the book contains some distortions because I have personal knowledge of some of the experiences that he distorts. For example, Timberman wrote that Minister Farrakhan made a trip to Libya in hopes of getting funds to support Reverend Jackson's presidential campaign. That statement is not true. Those of us who were involved in the trip know that it is not just a distortion but an outright lie.

The book is full of half-truths, distortions and outright lies; but one would ask, what is the purpose? After *The Enquirer*'s article on Jesse Jackson's extramarital newborn child and now this attack, perhaps Hilary Clinton's statement about a right-wing conspiracy attacking Bill Clinton is true. I believe another of its targets is Reverend Jackson.

I am critiquing this book not because I want people to read it. We need to have a demonstration against this type of literature. Black people should have a book-burning bonfire, exposing so-called journalists found guilty of trying to dismantle our leaders.

In Timberman's book, he uses Barbara Reynolds' book written in 1975 entitled, "America's David." I would like Ms. Reynolds, who is an excellent writer, to do a critique of how Timberman has used her name and work to further support his attack on Reverend Jackson.

If we allow people like Timberman to continue and do not lift up our voices, the Black community will have no leadership. People with the same view as Timberman will declare that all of our leadership is unworthy. We need to stand by our leaders.

51

New Book on the Honorable Elijah Muhammad: Truth Mixed With Falsehood and Outright Lies

The November 1999 edition of *Emerge* magazine convinced me that the editorial board led by George Curry, a man who at one time I respected as a responsible journalist, was not a friend of the Black struggle in America. He and his staff have failed to look into the accounts of events in the new book by Karl Evanzz, "The Rise and Fall of Elijah Muhammad." I accuse Curry and his staff of a miscarriage of justice when it comes to the fair and balanced treatment of a movement that has survived for 69 years in America.

The attack on the Nation of Islam and the personal character of the Honorable Elijah Muhammad is a tragedy for *Emerge* magazine and its publisher. I can speak like this because I lived through this period and was a part of this history. I am mentioned in the *Emerge* article under the name, "Larry 4X Prescott." I read the published treatment of Evanzz's forthcoming book. His first book on the Nation of Islam, "The Judas Factor," was a miserable failure and it appears that he is trying it again.

I can consider that Evanzz was either misguided, took it upon himself to fabricate his stories or, at worse, made a decision to just outright lie. If his source of information was from the FBI's Freedom of Information Act files.

AKBAR MUHAMMAD

I would hope that he would publish copies of the files with their file numbers so that those who know the facts can level their attacks against Evanzz and the FBI – a government organization that spends an enormous amount of money and time trying to destroy the Nation of Islam. The FBI and other government agencies are still working to undermine and destroy the work of Minister Louis Farrakhan. He has been blessed in the last 22 years to rebuild the Nation of Islam and bring honor and respect to the name of Elijah Muhammad.

If *Emerge* was doing a treatment of the book and its title is, "The Rise and Fall of Elijah Muhammad," why was there not a balance shown to reveal his rise and the good that he brought to Black America and the world? The treatment could then speak about the questionable areas of the noble life of the Honorable Elijah Muhammad.

I would like to take an aspect of the treatment given of the book as it appeared in *Emerge*, the truth to which I can personally attest. There are statements made by Evanzz as though he were in the room with the Honorable Elijah Muhammad and his family, or he was personally listening to copies of so-called tapes of conversations. There is no way that he would have had these experiences. Many of the people to whom he made reference in his book have passed away.

When he mentioned "the chickens coming home to roost," his facts are totally distorted. He writes:

> *"The Messenger was scheduled to speak in New York on Sunday, December 1 at Manhattan Center, but he fell ill a few days after the assassination, and was unable to travel. Naturally, Malcolm was the replacement."*

AFRICA AND THE WORLD: REVISITED

Moreover, he writes:

> "At the conclusion of his talk, Malcolm was questioned by a reporter, eager to know what he personally felt about Kennedy's death. Malcolm stuck to the script for a few minutes, but his compulsion to be true to himself overpowered his inclinations to obey Muhammad's order to tie his tongue in a knot."

The truth of the matter and circumstances that led up to this event at Manhattan Center on December 1, 1963 are as follows:

In September 1963, the Honorable Elijah Muhammad spoke to a packed auditorium in Philadelphia. The New York mosque organized 32 buses to travel to Philadelphia. At the end of the meeting, Malcolm came out to greet many of the brothers and sisters on the buses. I happened to be on the bus that he stepped on to announce that the Honorable Elijah Muhammad had agreed to come to New York in December.

We secured Manhattan Center on 34th Street for December 1st. We started planning this event weeks before President John F. Kennedy's assassination. When the death of President Kennedy was announced a few days later, the Honorable Elijah Muhammad suggested that we cancel the event.

On Wednesday, November 27th, Malcolm announced to the brothers and sisters at the mosque that the Honorable Elijah Muhammad instructed that we should make no comments regarding the death of President Kennedy. According to the words of Captain Yusef Shah (listed as Joseph X Gravitt in Evanzz's book), Malcolm was asked by the Honorable Elijah Muhammad to cancel. Malcolm explained that we could not get a refund nor could we change the date. So, the meeting was scheduled to go forward, with Malcolm as the speaker.

AKBAR MUHAMMAD

On December 1st, Captain Joseph X assigned Brother John D. X and me to escort Malcolm from his home in Queens to the Manhattan Center. In the car with Malcolm was also Sister Harriet Muhammad, wife of Akbar Muhammad, the youngest son of the Honorable Elijah Muhammad and Sister Clara Muhammad. She rode in the backseat. I could see Malcolm working his fingers as he would usually do as he taught. It was obvious that he was having a very involved conversation on the affairs of the Nation and the world.

When we arrived at the Manhattan Center, Captain Joseph was waiting to receive Malcolm with Malcolm's First Lieutenant, Clarence 7X. They reported to Malcolm that Mr. Handler from the *New York Times* was seeking admission to the meeting and that they had turned him away. This was based on the rule by the Honorable Elijah Muhammad after an incident in Flint, Michigan in October that year where a White policeman insisted on coming to our meeting with a firearm. The Honorable Elijah Muhammad said, from that day forward, he would not allow the press in our public meetings. (Details of this can be read in the book, "Message to the Blackman of America.")

Malcolm instructed Captain Joseph to get Mr. Handler, who had just walked away, and allow him in the meeting. At this point, Captain Joseph turned to Brother Clarence and told him to have Mr. Handler admitted to the meeting. Malcolm delivered an excellent and highly spirited lecture and, at the conclusion, he opened the floor for questions.

A Black man in a three-quarter jacket stood and asked Malcolm, "Would you comment on the death of President Kennedy?" Malcolm hesitated, as if he was in deep thought. There was a stillness in the auditorium that was almost frightening. When he finally spoke, his words were, "Being an old farm boy myself, chickens coming home to roost never made me sad – it always made me glad." The crowd broke out in a tremendous round of applause and Malcolm did not take any more questions.

AFRICA AND THE WORLD: REVISITED

When Malcolm left the Manhattan Center, Brother John and I remained on the detail to escort him back home. He drove up 8th Avenue into Central Park West and dropped off a young man, who was the son of Billy Eckstine.

Mr. Handler reported on Minister Malcolm's comment in the *New York Times* on Monday, December 2nd. And the very next day, Tuesday, December 3rd, the Honorable Elijah Muhammad asked Malcolm to suspend his public speaking until further notice.

There are enough men and women who are still alive who can assist anyone who is writing a book about the Honorable Elijah Muhammad so that the information shared with the reading public can be more factual, and not truth mixed falsehood and outright lies.

AKBAR MUHAMMAD

52

Remembering Marcus Garvey

On August 17th, we celebrated the 130th anniversary of Marcus Garvey's birth. Many of our young brothers and sisters only know the name Marcus Garvey and that he was a nationalist leader of a big organization in the early 1900s.

After being introduced to Marcus Garvey when a young man as I first came into the Nation of Islam, I always wondered to myself, "Why was not more knowledge of him and his contribution to our consciousness known among young people?" We should know more about this giant.

His preaching about Africa, Black self-love and consciousness allowed him to build the largest movement among Black people on the theme of Black consciousness. His life and movement will capture the reader. He started in Jamaica, where he was born, and moved throughout the Caribbean, Central America, United States and Canada.

By the time he ended up in New York, he had organized thousands of Black men and women and inspired young people at the time. As they marched through the streets of Harlem in beautiful uniforms, it inspired many of our young people as he preached the theme, "Africa for Africans at home and abroad."

When the Honorable Dr. Kwame Nkrumah, who led Ghana to its independence in 1957, was in a university in America, he studied Marcus Garvey and was inspired by him. It was this inspiration from Garvey that led to the Black star in the Ghanaian flag.

AKBAR MUHAMMAD

His life and work were important and it was the teacher of the Honorable Elijah Muhammad, Master Fard Muhammad who, in one of his letters to the Honorable Elijah Muhammad, encouraged him to mention Marcus Garvey in his speeches.

His movement was making such a tremendous impact in America and throughout the world that the government of America created some internal conflict within the movement that put them in position to arrest and deport Garvey. He died at the young age of 53 on June 10, 1940.

We who know the value of Marcus Garvey's life should know the importance of keeping his work alive across America and throughout the world. It takes more than just remembering Marcus Garvey on his birthday. It takes continuous discussion around what his philosophy was and his direction to connect us with our motherland Africa, as well as his emphasis on the importance of business in any movement to maintain independence.

As we celebrate 130 years of the birth of Mr. Garvey, we all should say in a strong voice, "Long live the spirit of Marcus Garvey! Long live the work of Marcus Garvey! Long live the inspiration of Marcus Garvey!"

53

Ghana In Transition:

When The Strong Man Goes

On December 7, 2000, the people of the Republic of Ghana will go to the polls to elect a new president. There has been much written about President Jerry Rawlings as he prepares to move on amid much controversy.

As a resident and friend of the people of Ghana for the last 10 years, I must say that, during the Rawlings Administration from the days of the Provisional National Defense Council (PNDC) to the National Democratic Congress (NDC), Ghana has enjoyed nearly 20 years of stability. Despite a fluctuating economy, Ghana remained peaceful. There were a few small internal problems in the northern region, but nothing on the scale of what we see in other African countries.

The June 4th Revolution brought pain to some people who lost loved ones, but there is a saying in the West, "I felt bad because I had no shoes until I met a man who had no feet."

Those who look at Ghana, who know Ghana, and love Ghana must put things on a scale. I am taught in my faith that, on the scale of justice, your good must outweigh your bad; and the ultimate Judge, knowing that man is not perfect and will make mistakes, will weigh your good deeds against those that are not so good. If your good carries the most weight, then you are rewarded accordingly.

AKBAR MUHAMMAD

I am not writing this article because President Rawlings has been a friend of the Nation of Islam and Minister Farrakhan, and I am not writing it because in 1986, President Rawlings opened the door for the Nation of Islam to establish its first office on the African continent. I am writing it because Africa needs our concern, love and involvement.

President Rawlings has given Ghana international recognition economically, politically and socially. Even those who disagree with his politics have to agree that, as a head of state, Rawlings has made a difference in Ghana.

It takes a certain strength and tenacity of will to be an effective head of state in Africa. Differences and disagreements are natural. It would be unnatural to agree with an individual on every point. However, the test is how disagreements are handled and managed. What we do not see in many African nations is the proper management of disagreements or points of view. A disagreement does not necessitate that the parties involved pick up weapons. They should instead come to a table and discuss the issues with a council, elders or those who have experience.

When we consider Africa and leaders such as former President Siad Barre in the country of Somalia, there were disagreements and some considered him a dictator. After Barre was overthrown, look at what occurred in Somalia. After years of civil war, killing, starvation and suffering, a new head of state is trying to unite the country. Many may have denounced Barre as a no-good dictator, but he had the strength to hold government together.

When the strong man at the center steps down or is removed, those who come behind him should take his good and build on it. They should accentuate the positive, instead of focusing solely on his negatives, and not condemn the man or those who went before him. Another African nation where there is much chaos and strife is the Cote d'Ivoire, just next door to Ghana. Again, it takes a certain type of strength for a leader on the African continent to hold a society together.

AFRICA AND THE WORLD: REVISITED

I am hopeful that my brother and friend President Rawlings will use his expertise to help Ghana and Africa. As he steps away from the awesome responsibility of president, I hope those who come behind him (from either political party) will council with him, get his views and, yes, even take his advice, given his experiences and successes holding Ghana together over the past 20 years.

It would be foolish to reinvent the wheel and not consider Rawlings' experiences for the sake of Ghana. I have met Ghanaians all over the world, and I can say without a doubt that I have not met one that disliked his country. There is a love for one's country and the soil that nourished them. This same love is with President Rawlings.

I would hope that his memoir would be a book that would contain not only a record of what he has done, but also a record of his experiences. This is a turning point for Ghana.

When a strong man goes, those that step behind him are tested. Can they hold that society together and can they move it forward in a manner that will continue to serve its people's needs? So we ask that God's blessing and guidance go with our President Jerry John Rawlings, his family and the people of Ghana.

AKBAR MUHAMMAD

54

STAND UP FOR PRESIDENT ROBERT MUGABE

The entire Black world should stand up for President Robert Mugabe. Around the world, people from Japan to Argentina, from Ireland to New Zealand, from Canada to Mexico, and across Africa have all read about Robert Mugabe. The picture that is painted in the press controlled by America, Europe and others is of a 78-year-old dictator trying to hold onto power. It is said that he is threatening and condoning the beating of White farmers in order to take their land, which is causing his people to starve. These stories have been played and replayed.

The Black world should consider the other side of this story. Here is a war hero who is still strong and vigorous, with a clear mind and determined idea to do what is right. He could have been swayed by world opinion and weak African leaders who only want to appear as "good boys" for Europe and America. He could be swayed by the idea of democracy and an opposition party that is bought and paid for by the White farmers, England and, yes, even America. Yet, he has stayed the course. For this reason, the Black world should stand up for President Mugabe.

AKBAR MUHAMMAD

How do we show our support? First, by beginning a mass letter writing campaign from concerned Africans at home and abroad. The letters can be addressed as follows:

His Excellency Robert Mugabe

President of the Republic of Zimbabwe

State House

Harare, Zimbabwe (Africa)

We should let him know that there are those in the Black/African world who separate the truth from propaganda. We clearly understand what we are seeing and hearing. We also know something about the objectives of those who oppose what is just and right. We feel that true justice is the return of land to the African people. This is what is troubling the Western world, because it causes them to look at their own history and injustices.

A review of history tells us of the first White settlers who came to what is now called Zimbabwe in 1890. It was Cecil Rhodes who sent more than 200 farmers, miners, soldiers and others, whom he called the pioneer column. He also sent 300 policemen from Johannesburg under what was called the British South African Company. His objective was to find gold and expand British influence, according to the writings of historian Dr. Henry Louis Gates.

They found little gold, and thus turned to farming and cattle ranching. The settlers began forcing Africans from the land onto tribal reserves. Therefore, this land that is in question today is land that was stolen from the Africans when those who came looking for gold and mineral riches did not find them, but instead they found fertile land that could be farmed and used for cattle-raising.

The African leaders of Zimbabwe turned to the British crown for protection against this design. However, England gave Rhodes the green light and he continued to take land from Africans. He renamed the land, "Rhodesia," after himself. To add insult to injury, they began to impose taxes on the Africans, which had to be paid in cash or kind. This is when the first rebellion against White rule began, and lasted from 1896 to 1897. This rebellion against White occupation, robbery and oppression of the African people was brutally suppressed. There were no other rebellions until the war of liberation began in the early 1960s.

As the question of land in Zimbabwe is at the top of the news, someone needs to take a moment to review the history of not only how the land was stolen from the people, but also their cattle and crops. In the 1930s, Whites who controlled the country allotted land according to race. As a result, Whites ended up with most of the land. They displaced Black people on native reserves. Black people were allowed few educational opportunities. Instead, they received a form of vocational training similar to what took place in America for Blacks who were primarily trained to be serviceable to White America. In Zimbabwe, African people were trained to be serviceable to the White colonial settlers who robbed their land.

Labor conditions and wages were below standard, as was typical whenever White settlers occupied land owned by Africans. They paid them the lowest wages for the hardest work. Not only did they keep the wages low, but trade unions were forbidden in domestic services, mining and agriculture. These are the three largest sectors of employment in the country of Zimbabwe.

Those who are not old enough to remember should be taught the history of when the British saw the handwriting on the wall. They granted independence to northern Rhodesia and Nyasaland, which are now Zambia and Malawi. Yet, it was the hardcore Whites of southern Rhodesia, under the leadership of Ian Smith, who resisted and fought a bitter battle for independence to maintain their oppressive rule over Black people.

AKBAR MUHAMMAD

The battle and struggle for land lasted until independence came to Africans in April 1980. It has always been about the question of land - land that belonged to the African people. To have fought this long struggle for the rights to their own land that was stolen from them, but depicted as a brute force because they are taking land from "innocent" Whites is far from the truth.

Many do not know of the long struggle of Mugabe, who spent nearly 10 years in prison. He also lived and taught in Ghana, the birthplace of his first wife, Sally. Many do not know of his years in Tanzania and its ongoing struggle until independence. Few know about the negotiations at the Lancaster House, where America and England made promises and then broke them. There should be no question about what side the African world should stand on when it comes to the question of land in Zimbabwe.

Black Americans have similar circumstances. Seventy years ago in America, Black people owned approximately 16 million acres of land. Now, according to what I learned at the Reparations March, we are down to approximately three million acres. Most of this land was stolen from us through unjust laws and practices. In Mississippi, there was a law that, if your mother and father owned 1,000 acres of land and they passed away, the land would be divided among the descendants. If one of the descendants decided to sell his/her portion, then all of the land had to be sold. Also, the local government would not send appropriate tax information to Black landowners, and a year later they would present them with a summons claiming that their land was sold for back taxes.

The land question in Zimbabwe is clear, for the land belongs to the Africans. It was stolen from them and should be returned to them. Now, after fighting a war of liberation over their land, the land should be returned to them. The Black/African world should stand with Mugabe. All of those African presidents who have lifted their voices to condemn their brother should receive a letter from the African world. They should be told that, if they disagree with their brother and they do not have anything good to say about him, it is better in the face of attacks from Europe and America that they save their comments and speak to him in private!

We must stand with President Robert Mugabe and the land reforms in the country of Zimbabwe. As our nationalist brothers and sisters in America say, "Free The Land!"

AKBAR MUHAMMAD

55

The Death of General Sani Abacha

By Askia Muhammad and Akbar Muhammad

General Sani Abacha's untimely death in Nigeria leaves a great vacuum, not only in his native land, but in all of West Africa and, indeed, throughout the African continent. Nigeria has the largest population in Africa, with 115 million people. One in every five Africans is a Nigerian. The country has wealth as a result of oil exports; and with the largest standing army on the continent, was a stabilizing force. In times of trouble, General Abacha stood in the breach and worked tirelessly to hold his country together. Even those who disagreed with him must acknowledge his role in maintaining the unity of Nigeria.

"We found him to be a great listener, and he showed great interest in our opinions," said Dorothy Leavell, president of the National Newspaper Publishers Association (NNPA), the Black press of America. This is hardly the description of a man so many have labeled a "dictator." Ms. Leavell, as a leader of numerous delegations of Black publishers and observers, met with General Abacha on many occasions. The group monitored elections and the democratization process that General Abacha promised to conclude with the installation of a democratically elected civilian government by October 1, 1998.

If Nigeria follows the record of General Abacha's leadership in the crisis in Liberia – where Nigeria helped Liberia maintain stability long enough for national elections and the installation of a civilian government which has begun the reunification and reconstruction in Liberia after seven years of civil war – then Nigeria may see peace and stability at the end of its own transition process.

It was U.S. President George Bush, Secretary of Defense Dick Cheney and Joint Chief of Staff General Colin Powell who conferred on General Abacha the Legion of Merit's degree of commander, known as the Distinguished Service Star – the highest U.S. military honor. In the 1991 commendation, Secretary Cheney said of General Abacha, "His personal efforts during a crisis in Liberia and direct support of the Economic Community Monitoring Group (ECOMOG) and Economic Community of West African States (ECOWAS) operations ensured the humanitarian treatment of both civilian and military forces, who brought the conflict to a rapid conclusion and established law and order during a period of total anarchy."

If Nigeria follows the record of General Abacha's leadership in the crisis in neighboring Sierra Leone – where Nigeria helped restore the civilian elected president to power after a coup by a junior army officer – then Nigeria must certainly reestablish and restore its own civilian governing authority.

We and all true friends of Africa and Nigeria sincerely hope that Nigeria's new leader will continue the path of transition to civilian rule with minimum delay. We offer our heartfelt condolences to General Abacha's widow Maryam Abacha. Hers is an especially great loss because she also lost her son Ibrahim, who died in a plane crash less than two years ago.

56

The Death of Laurent Kabila:

The Man Who Wouldn't Be America's Boy

The tragic death of Laurent Kabila, president of the Congo, is a setback not only for the Democratic Republic of the Congo, but for all of Africa. You can conclude from the writings in the Western press that he was not a favorite of America or certain European powers. In the newspapers and magazines that I have read, whenever the Ugandan and Rwandan troops' presence in the Congo was mentioned, it was never mentioned where these soldiers received their backing.

The world is aware that there is fighting and dying occurring in the Congo, but the reason is not generally known. At the root of much of the killing and suffering that is taking place is the presence of foreign troops. The tragedy is that the Ugandan and Rwandan troops initially fought to remove the late President Kabila, and subsequently they turned on each other. A double tragedy is that both the Ugandan and Rwandan troops are sponsored and many are trained by the U.S. government.

AKBAR MUHAMMAD

Ironically, in the late President Kabila's obituaries from different parts of the world, many of the writers chose to talk about his personal life during the 30 years he spent challenging the late Joseph Sese Seko Mobutu's government. Again, none of the newspapers mentioned that he was struggling against a brutal dictator who was backed and propped up by the U.S. government. The Congo (formerly Zaire) has a long-standing relationship of 36 years with America (1961-1997), with the support of six American presidents.

Of the many things that Belgium and America feared from Kabila is that he would one day ask for compensation from Belgium and the family of King Leopold for the exploitation of the resources of the Congo and the enslavement of its citizens from 1890-1906. During this brutal period, many men and women had their limbs severed, in particular their hands, for not working hard enough on the plantations. The end result was the murder of hundreds, thousands, if not millions of the people of the Congo. You may recall the horrific pictures of the skulls of our Black brothers and sisters of the Congo stacked in a pyramid with a White Belgium officer standing in front of them.

Now, America is concerned about being charged with the death of Patrice Lumumba, the first prime minister of the Congo after colonial rule. Although in recent years, there has been an attempt to shift the responsibility to the Belgium secret service, we know now that the CIA was directed to kill Lumumba. This has been directly verified from the writings of one of its own secret agents. America is also concerned about the mounting evidence of her medical experiments on the Congolese people. In the early 1970s, a book was published entitled, "Who Killed The Congo?" Today, that question can be answered: America, Belgium and France.

When the diaries of the Cuban revolutionary leader Ernesto "Che" Guevara were published in 1999, he mentioned Kabila, whom he met when he was in the Congo helping in their struggle against the American-backed dictator Mobutu. In Kabila's obituary, printed in

AFRICA AND THE WORLD: REVISITED

The Economist magazine, it quoted Guevara's book, which was very derogatory about Kabila, as saying that Kabila was not serious.

If I had anything to add to the obituary, I would have added that Guevara put the thought and buried it deep in Kabila's mind: "Never trust the Americans." When Kabila came to power in 1997, he reflected on this, by never allowing the Americans to get too close to him. He made it next to impossible for America to make him their "boy" as had been done to Mobutu.

Our late, departed brother backed the new initiative of Brother Muammar Qadhafi on the United States of Africa. Kabila felt that, if we would unite Africa, the riches of the Congo could help build Africa. In the past, those riches helped build Europe and America. The problems of the Congo and the ongoing war between the legitimate government in Kinshasa and the American-backed Rwandan and Ugandan troops, could come to an end if America directs its puppets to leave the Congo so that they can find a peaceful solution.

When Kabila came into power, he promised democratic elections in four years. In knowing Africa, I personally believe that was a reasonable timeframe. Since he did not "buck dance" for America or allow her entities into the country to once again exploit it, he was criticized and attacked. Consequently, America financed troops to overthrow his government.

May God be pleased with our brother Laurent Kabila, a man who refused to be America's boy.

AKBAR MUHAMMAD

X
LAW & JUSTICE:
THE EFFICACY OF REPARATIONS AND PRISONER RESETTLEMENT

Akbar Muhammad conducting a slave dungeon tour of the Cape Coast Castle in Ghana (2013) L-R Abdul Usman, Kofi, Akbar Muhammad, Jehron Muhammad

57
Reparations Take Center Stage

For many years, the Black American community in North America and other Africans in the Diaspora, specifically in Canada, the Caribbean and South America, have written and talked about receiving reparations from European and American nations that have benefited from the institution of slavery. However, until now, our audiences have been limited and our appeals have been marginalized.

The United Nations will hold a conference in Durban, South Africa from August 31-September 8, 2001 entitled, "The World Conference Against Racism." For this conference, non-governmental organizations (NGOs) and others have been pushing to have the Trans-Atlantic Slave Trade declared a crime against humanity and move straight to the discussion on reparations. America has threatened to boycott the conference if this language and discussion are not changed. They also threatened to boycott if the conference has a platform to declare Zionism as racism.

AKBAR MUHAMMAD

The topic of reparations started a long time ago in America and it has always tried to circumvent the issue. The Honorable Elijah Muhammad has been an advocate of reparations for the descendants of slavery. However, he did not consistently use the word "reparations." He put his position in writing 40 years ago in 1961 when the *Muhammad Speaks* newspaper presented the Nation of Islam's program under the title of "What The Muslims Want and What The Muslims Believe." In 1979, when Minister Louis Farrakhan began to rebuild the Nation of Islam, he placed the same program in *The Final Call* newspaper.

There may be points on the Nation of Islam's reparations program with which others in the reparations movement may disagree. We have the right to disagree, yet our goal for reparations must still remain the same. What we ask for, how we ask for it, and when and where are issues that can be discussed down the road as we move along this journey.

When reading the points that the Honorable Elijah Muhammad raised on reparations, they state:

> "1) We want freedom. We want a full and complete freedom.
>
> 2) We want justice. Equal justice under the law. We want justice applied equally to all, regardless of creed or class or color.
>
> 3) We want equality of opportunity. We want equal membership in society with the best in civilized society.
>
> 4) We want our people in America whose parents or grandparents were descendants from slaves to be allowed to establish a separate state or territory of their own – either on this continent or elsewhere. We believe that our former slave masters are obligated to provide such land and that the area must be fertile and minerally rich. We believe that our former slave masters are obligated to maintain and supply our needs in this separate territory for the next 20 to 25 years – until we

are able to produce and supply our own needs."

These four points are basically the Honorable Elijah Muhammad's position on reparations. However, point number five reads:

> "We want freedom for all Believers of Islam now held in federal prisons. We want freedom for all Black men and women now under death sentence in innumerable prisons in the North as well as the South."

This does not just pertain to Muslims, but it pertains to all Black men and women. On the land issue, it reads,

> "We want every Black man and woman to have the freedom to accept or reject being separated from the slave master's children and establish a land of their own."

As you read on to point number seven, the Honorable Elijah Muhammad states,

> "As long as we are not allowed to establish a state or territory of our own, we demand not only equal justice under the laws of the United States, but equal employment opportunities – NOW!"

Then, he goes on to say,

> "We do not believe that after 400 years of free or nearly free labor, sweat and blood, which has helped America become rich and powerful, that so many thousands of Black people should have to subsist on relief, charity or live in poor houses."

He then continues with another point of his reparations program:

> "We want the government of the United States to exempt our people from ALL taxation as long as we are deprived of equal justice under the laws of the land."

AKBAR MUHAMMAD

Those who have been involved in the reparations struggle for years, i.e. the National Coalition of Blacks for Reparations in America (N'COBRA), should be happy that reparations have taken center stage worldwide and is now in the forefront of the hearts and minds of our people. Many of those who did not have any idea of what the word reparations meant at one time are now echoing our call for reparations on many different levels.

We must take the words from Amiri Baraka (Leroi Jones) when, during the height of our struggle in 1972, he challenged us with the phrase "unity in diversity." On the question of reparations, there must be unity on this proposition, though there is diversity in terms of our approach.

I do not think that those of us in the reparations movement should condemn or abandon Randall Robinson for his book, "The Debt." His efforts should be applauded because he took the time to research and write it. We should thank David Horowitz for his newspaper articles across the country, in particular his articles that reached the college campus newspapers. He brought us together as never before, to condemn him and his madness of why we should not receive reparations. Our students responded by saying he had the audacity to tell us we do not deserve reparations and then try to divide us on the issue.

We should work together to get our churches, mosques and temples involved in the proposition of reparations. Each of them could have study groups at least once a month to discuss reparations. I strongly suggest that, after the conference in South Africa, we have a three-day national convention on reparations and bring thousands of our people into a location to discuss reparations. The conference should be held in America, the Caribbean and then Africa. We need to bring all of the various views to the table. Next, we should issue a solid, united platform for the governments of America and Europe to address.

AFRICA AND THE WORLD: REVISITED

We hope that this conference in South Africa will be the beginning. This is a good opportunity for many of the reparations committees, organizations, religious and secular societies who have lobbied for reparations to now have a worldwide platform.

We should thank President George Bush for opposing the conference's platform to declare the Trans-Atlantic Slave Trade a crime against humanity and the need for reparations. He is helping us marshal our forces across the country. He has made it an issue in areas where it would have never been brought up before. As we can see in the August 27th edition of *Newsweek* magazine, there are six full pages on the issue of reparations. Bush has helped make it a dinner table conversation, where formerly we have never had a conversation on the proposition of reparations.

We thank the forerunners of this proposition. Some of us have worked in this vineyard for many years; and although others may be getting all the recognition, we should continue to support them. It does not matter who has been recognized. The objective of what we are trying to accomplish is the point. Reparations must remain center stage.

AKBAR MUHAMMAD

58

Apologies Are In Order

Recently, who saw throughout the world that President Bill Clinton apologized for the horrible Tuskegee Experiment that lasted 40 years. If the experiment had lasted for two to five years, and the government said it was a terrible thing that was organized by a few misguided American scientists who were racist to the core and had no regard for Black people whatsoever, we could only say that the government of America is true to form and does not only lie sometimes, but lies all the time. However, when the experiment lasts 40 years, starting in the early thirties and ending in the early seventies, then we know that there were more than just a few misguided scientists involved.

This Tuskegee Experiment with syphilis gave credibility to the rumors of how the AIDS virus was started and directed toward minorities, in particular Black people of Africa.

President Clinton stood before an audience of the descendants and relatives of those who suffered and died under this terrible experiment and apologized for the wickedness of his government. If he was offering a sincere apology not only to those families, but to the Black community of America, why would he bring one of the survivors, one who has the heart to forgive and forget, and make it appear as if White folks did not really mean to do that to us, and that we accept their apology. Well, if this is the reason for apologies, then why doesn't Clinton keep going?

AKBAR MUHAMMAD

He should first apologize for slavery and what slavery brought to the Black community. He should apologize for the aftermath of slavery, the 40 acres and the mule that was promised to each former slave by President Andrew Jackson. He should apologize for the making of this pledge and his government's reneging on the pledge.

He should apologize for the growth of segregation and the mistreatment of Black people. He should apologize for our not being allowed to vote or become properly educated. He should apologize for the abuse that we suffered at the hands of White folks on plantations as sharecroppers (they were really glorified slaves for the company store).

He should apologize for the suffering that Blacks faced after World War I; and for the Brownsville, Texas soldiers who went to Europe and helped America win the war against the Germans, and then came home only to be lynched by Americans. He should apologize for these Americans who put them to death.

He should apologize for our mistreatment during World War II, where Blacks were segregated and yet used as a fighting force. Blacks were used in the most menial tasks, e.g. in the Navy we cooked and washed the decks. He should apologize for the actions of the American people and, yes, the American government. He should apologize for those soldiers who returned home after the war, only to suffer mistreatment, being last hired and first fired.

He is old enough to remember the suffering that took place during the civil rights struggle in America. He should apologize to the King family for their grief regarding all the unanswered questions concerning the assassination of Dr. Martin Luther King Jr. Maybe a wider investigation may lead to exposing the U.S. government as the hand behind his assassination. He should apologize in advance before it comes to light.

AFRICA AND THE WORLD: REVISITED

While President Clinton is apologizing for these things, he should also apologize for the way that the CIA handles itself across the African continent. He should apologize for using a Black man from America in Ghana to help overthrow Dr. Kwame Nkrumah and bring down a regime that meant so much to the entire African continent, and destroying the aspirations of so many in the process.

He should apologize for his CIA operations in Liberia and propping up the regimes of Liberia that catered to the interests of the United States and a few of its people. The destruction that Liberia is still suffering to this day has America at the root of it.

In addition, President Clinton should apologize for Joseph Mobutu, whom the American government paid, supported and kept in power, knowing that he was exploiting the wealth of his country; knowing that he did not allow democracy in Zaire; and knowing that he was on the CIA payroll. Clinton should apologize for allowing bases to be set up in Zaire to aid the National Union for the Total Independence of Angola (UNITA). He should apologize for the landmines made in America that have maimed and crippled thousands of innocent people in Angola.

In the book, "Killing Hope: U.S. Military and CIA Interventions Since World War II" by William Blum, the author mentions some of these things for which America needs to apologize, if apologies are in order.

One only needs to look at the list of evil deeds, which includes the killing of Patrice Lumumba in 1961 in the Democratic Republic of the Congo (formerly Zaire); the attempt to kill Sheikh Mohammad Hussein Fadlallah in Lebanon, where 80 people were killed in that attempt; the attempt to kill Muammar Qadhafi in 1986 in Libya, where more than 100 innocent people lost their lives in this assassination attempt; the attempt in 1976 to assassinate the late Prime Minister Michael Manley of Jamaica because of his relationship with Fidel Castro of Cuba; and the many attempts to kill Fidel Castro since 1960; to know that apologies are in order.

AKBAR MUHAMMAD

The government of America needs to apologize to the Black communities, for there is overwhelming evidence that America was involved in allowing crack cocaine to be smuggled into the U.S. from Central America to be sold in the Black communities, with the CIA's involvement. We deserve an apology.

The President needs to apologize for a justice system that has more than 1.5 million men and women who are incarcerated in the prisons of America today. He needs to apologize for letting the so-called "free enterprise system" open private prisons where people can buy shares on the stock market to better facilitate the warehousing of Black men and women.

Black and minority students who, because of the elimination of many affirmative action programs, now have diminished possibilities for getting a decent education, deserve an apology.

Therefore, Mr. President, if this is the season of apologies, you need to reassess just apologizing for the terrible Tuskegee Experiment. I believe that the Pope led the way when he said that the Western world needs to apologize for participating in the horrors of the slave trade. Behind the apology, however, there need to be actions to show that the apology is really sincere. This means more than building a $200,000 facility in Tuskegee, Alabama. It goes far beyond that, if this really is the season for apologies.

59

WHY IS IT SO DIFFICULT FOR PRESIDENT CLINTON TO APOLOGIZE FOR SLAVERY?

On President Bill Clinton's recent African tour – which indeed was a historical trip for an American president to visit the heart of Africa – he mentioned slavery and the descendants of slavery, but he never officially apologized for America's role in slavery.

By President Clinton not apologizing for America's participation in the Trans-Atlantic Slave Trade, he missed an opportunity to go down in history as the American president who was big enough, wise enough and courageous enough to apologize for America enslaving millions of Black men and women from Africa.

When we pick up newspapers and read about P.W. Botha in his defiance of the Truth and Reconciliation Commission and his sheer arrogance in dealing with the truth of the apartheid regime and its misdeeds against the whole Black population, one would wonder why it took the world so long to come to the point of condemning apartheid in South Africa. Botha refuses to apologize for his role in apartheid or the role of any of those around him. America should be seen in the same light, when around the world there is pressure for governments and people to apologize for past misdeeds.

The Germans are an example. The present generation of Germans were not the ones who persecuted and attempted to exterminate the Jewish people; but as their children, they are busy apologizing and even paying reparations to Jewish people and the Jewish state.

AKBAR MUHAMMAD

The pressures that have been put on Japan from the Koreans, especially the Korean women who were held as sex slaves by the Japanese during World War II. These so-called "comfort women" are pressing the Japanese government for an official apology and compensation.

The 120,000 Japanese Americans who were put in concentration camps in America after the bombing of Pearl Harbor pressed the U.S. government for an apology and compensation, and received both. British soldiers recently protested the Japanese Emperor's visit to England, demanding an official apology for the treatment of British POW solders during World War II.

The Germans have admitted their wrong in Namibia from 1902-1907 in their attempt to exterminate an entire group of Black Namibians. They recently discussed an apology and their attempt to compensate those who were wronged by the actions of the Germans. The present generation of Germans was not alive nor many of their fathers, but they must shoulder the responsibility.

Armenians have pressed the Turks for an apology for what they say is the Turks' responsibility for the death of 1.5 million Armenians. On a visit in the early 1990s to Cote d'Ivoire, the Pope said that Europeans should apologize to Africans for their participation in the slave trade. The United States of America, which benefited most from the slave trades, a country where the descendants of those slaves still suffer daily, refuses for some reason to apologize.

The statement made by President Yoweri Museveni of Uganda, before the visit of President Clinton, was a statement that was distasteful, untimely, unnecessary and unwarranted. Museveni said, as reported by the *BBC* all across Africa, "There is no need for President Clinton to apologize for slavery. If anyone should apologize, it should be the kings and leaders who sold the slaves to the Europeans and others." This statement is unnecessary and only helps Europeans and Americans who participated in this Black Holocaust to say, "We enslaved you, but it really was not our fault; it was the fault of the Africans who sold you to us."

AFRICA AND THE WORLD: REVISITED

This argument keeps surfacing and many insensitive Africans support this position, which gives Europeans and White Americans an "out" regarding reparations and apologizing. The line of reasoning is, "If you want to sue anyone over slavery, you need to start with the African chiefs, kings and leaders who sold your people to us." America should officially apologize for slavery. If there are any doubts in the minds of African Americans regarding an apology for slavery, I suggest a thorough reading of any material pertaining to the treatment of slaves and their families, particularly those books and articles written by slave owners (e.g. "Slaves in the Family" by Edward Ball).

Is the fear of an apology centered around Black people asking for reparations? If the Southern Baptists could ask for forgiveness, then certainly the government of America, which legalized slavery and allowed it to be sustained in this country, should apologize for its participation, role and sanctioning of this heinous crime. Millions of Black people are suffering from residuals of slavery.

As I write this article, perhaps President Clinton's advisers should suggest that, instead of Clinton leaving a legacy of alleged indiscretions with women, he should leave a legacy that will overshadow these indiscretions. His legacy could read: "Although Clinton is a southerner from a former slave state, he grew up to become a leader of this country and decided it was time to officially apologize to the African American population for the role that America played in slavery." This could be the legacy of President William Jefferson Clinton, instead of Kenneth Star and Monica Lewinsky.

AKBAR MUHAMMAD

60

CORRECTING A HISTORICAL WRONG: THE STRUGGLE FOR QUOTAS

After the controversy over the University of Michigan's affirmative action program and the Trent Lott debacle, it is clear that President George Bush is a politician playing to White folks. He knows the way that many White Americans feel about affirmative action.

Into this picture, I have not heard one politician mention correcting the historical wrong of slavery. We suffered an unjust policy that they wrote into the laws of this country. White America justified the enslavement of Black people because of the color of our skin. It was written in the United States Constitution that a Black was three-fifths of a human being; it is like putting us in a race, breaking both of our legs and expecting us to run just as fast as everyone else. Set asides and affirmative action are the best ways that America can correct a historical wrong. Black people are waking up to a reality that we are due and justified reparations. This is another way to take back anything that would be owed to us for the wrong in bringing our foreparents out of Africa in the bowels of slave ships.

Millions died in the Middle Passage; the rest suffered on plantations while they were dehumanized, stripped of their humanity and culture. Our women were raped. White men sometimes enslaved the children they fathered through our women. This is a historical wrong. And America has a responsibility to God, the country and our people to correct this wrong. So, affirmative action and quota systems that favor the descendants of slaves are justified, especially from a government and its people who are fighting against just reparations.

President Bush, who is about to enter a war, is calling on young Blacks, Hispanics and American Indians to participate in the war and possibly die. In the middle of this, he states that he is opposed to affirmative action. His opposition to the University of Michigan's admission program that favors Blacks and Hispanics is an insult to the African American community, Hispanic community and American Indian community. Does he have another method to correct the historical wrong of the mistreatment of our people in this country? We face racism every day that we live in America – in jobs, hospitals and the military.

His position shows his level of insult and insensitivity – depending on many of our people not thinking about the historical wrongs committed against us in this country. Not only the Congressional Black Caucus, but every church in America should lift up its voice on Sunday morning. Every mosque in America should lift up its voice, as well as every temple and civic organization. President Bush should get emails, letters and phone calls to the White House.

The question that they should ask is, "How much insult should we take?" There are many Black men and women in this country who are in key positions because of affirmative action, set asides and the quota system.

61

AN APPEAL TO REVEREND JESSE JACKSON: WORK TO LIBERATE THE OTHER CAPTIVES

As I sat and watched Reverend Jesse Jackson on television in North Africa, I was proud and inspired at his courageous effort in liberating the three American prisoners of war in the Balkans.

No one can deny that Reverend Jackson has a keen sense of timing, an ability to analyze a given circumstance and bring clarity to the situation in a manner in which both a person "of letters" or "no letters" can see and understand. No one can deny Reverend Jackson's profound ability to think on his feet and give the right spiritual, political, social and economic input in any given case.

When Reverend Jackson invited Minister Louis Farrakhan to go to Syria to liberate the pilot, Robert Goodman, I was honored to travel with them. We watched Reverend Jackson work, and even those who disagree with him at times were extremely proud of the way that he handled that victory. His talents were further demonstrated when he handled President Ronald Reagan, who did not want to give him credit for his victory upon returning to America. We watched him in Cuba with Brother Fidel Castro, and in Geneva with Mikhail Gorbachev. However, charity begins at home and spreads abroad.

AKBAR MUHAMMAD

My appeal to my brother, Reverend Jackson, is the suffering of the 1.8 million captives in the jails of America, of which 80 percent are Black, Hispanic, American Indian and other minorities. Many are inmates on death row and many are serving excessive amounts of time. Yes, some have been involved in criminal and anti-social activities that are detrimental to American society and way of life. However, we must consider this reality in light of their plight in America and the injustices they have suffered because of the color of their skin. The residuals of slavery still affect every aspect of Black life in America.

God has blessed Reverend Jackson to have the ears of the rulers of this land. Our brothers and sisters in the prisons of America do not have the means to work with the power structure of America. What if you, Reverend Jackson, could repatriate to Africa some of our brothers and sisters who are languishing in the prisons of America. Many have become believers, some in Christianity, some in Islam. Many have educated themselves. We can try an alternative to death row and inordinate prison sentences. What does American society have to lose?

If Reverend Jackson and other concerned religious and political leaders would approach some of the leaders in Africa who have tremendous land area and small populations, probably they would consider this idea. The money spent to warehouse these brothers and sisters ($20,000 - $52,000 a year for one inmate) can maintain them for a while in Africa. With the privatization of prisons and selling of shares by corporations on Wall Street, I say we must do something.

I want to close this appeal by recalling a petition made by a Nigerian living in Louisiana, USA to the current head of state of Nigeria, General Abdul Salam Abubakar. This Nigerian would like to see his government show an interest in the plight of imprisoned Nigerians throughout the Diaspora and work to bring them home. He feels this can be accomplished by negotiating with the governments holding Nigerians in prison in their countries.

Let us take a page from American history and free the captive believers. In the early days of American history, the British freed their prisoners and sent them to America and Australia to build a new reality in a strange land. Give these contemporary prisoners a new lease on life on a continent that needs many of the skills we have acquired in our 400-year sojourn in the West, not the criminal skills adopted from our former slave masters, but our humane and nation-building skills. Let the work begin to free the captive believers.

AKBAR MUHAMMAD

AFRICA AND THE WORLD: REVISITED

62

CAN AFRICA HELP AMERICA SOLVE ITS PRISON PROBLEM?

The November 13, 2000 edition of *Newsweek* magazine had a cover story by Ellis Cose entitled, "America's Prison Generation." He stated that 14 million Americans, mainly Black and Hispanic, will spend a part of their lives behind prison walls. The question we must ask is, "Why is America putting more and more young Blacks and Hispanics in jail? Just as they talk about Generation X, Drug Culture and Baby Boomers, we now have a Prison Generation. The questions are: Why? What can we do to stop it? What can we do for those who are incarcerated?

For many years, I have read and thought about the possibility of relocating some of our prisoners, who are actually victims of a wicked, oppressive system – a system that has, in reality, broken both of their legs yet expects them to run the race of life on equal par with those who have two healthy legs. How is it that America, who is enjoying the best prosperity in its history, has the largest prison population in the world? This, in spite of the fact that America does not have the largest population in the world.

AKBAR MUHAMMAD

At one time, it was said that the prison populations in China and Russia were greater than America's. But when you look at the population of China, there is no comparison to the population of America. I am not aware of any statistics that prove China has more than two million people in its prisons. We have to wonder if the figure of two million that is circulated in the press represents those who are in local jails waiting for bond and those waiting to go on trial. If we take those individuals into consideration, the figure would be even higher.

We need a radical new solution to the problem of the prisons in America. The solution should come from Black elected officials on the federal, state and local levels of government because the majority of the prison population are Black and Hispanic people.

In 1986 in New Orleans, Minister Louis Farrakhan proposed that we look at resettling prisoners in Africa. The common response would be, "How would it work? Africa has enough problems." In the book, "The Negotiation" by Gilbert White, the people had to select a Black leader who would negotiate with the American government on the issue of separation. Black Americans want to select a Black leader or a council of Black leaders who could negotiate with the American government and African governments to have prisoners released to the African continent.

In a *Time* magazine article, a writer says that no one has seriously suggested that America throw open the jailhouse doors. However, victims have a right to justice and society must protect itself from those who would rob, rape and, otherwise, violate the innocent. Therefore, prisons will always have a place in a civilized world.

We have much to consider. Most of the prisoners in America are descendants of the slaves who were brought out of Africa in the horrors of the Trans-Atlantic Slave Trade. Most of the prisoners are descendants of those were never given an equal chance in this society.

AFRICA AND THE WORLD: REVISITED

We must look at what capitalism, in its raw form, has done to a whole nation of people. We must look at the disparities between the haves and the have-nots in this society. We must consider the vicious cycle of poverty, where entire generations repeat the cycle. Then, we must ask ourselves: Why are so many Black people in jail? Do they have criminal mentalities or have they not been taught properly or given the proper opportunities to use their God-given abilities to make a way in the world?

Let's look at some of the possibilities of how this could work, First, in the prisons of America, among the Black Americans, Hispanics and American Indians are brilliant young men and women – many of whom are self-taught, without a formal education. However, they have many skills that are being squandered or wasted away in prison.

We can begin with negotiations with some of the governments in Africa that have tremendous land areas and small populations. America is now paying from $22,000 to $24,000 a year, and maybe as high as $50,000 a year for one inmate. If the government wants to save money and not use the prison system as a private entity, as well as eliminate the abuse factors associated with privatization, Africa is a reasonable consideration. The public never hears about the riots, bad food and mistreatment of inmates, which only recently came to the surface. Most information of this nature has been suppressed and kept out of the press.

If we say that we want to save the American taxpayers' money, then why not negotiate with some of the African governments? Give them the money to take some of our prisoners, especially those who have been reformed in prison and have been serving long sentences. It is inhumane to put a man or woman in prison for 25-30 years for a crime that does not involve murder. Many of those who have been convicted of murder are reformed. They may have made mistakes as teenagers due to immaturity. America must do something different.

AKBAR MUHAMMAD

We can negotiate with African governments and ask them for land areas where we can build colonies or small settlements, where these prisoners can go and work out a new reality. If the state or federal government is of the opinion that these individuals are a burden or menace to society, then offer them a deal. If a prisoner accepts the move to Africa and they are serving time for a heinous crime, they can never come back to America. I feel that many of our young brothers and sisters who are doing 50 or 60 years in prisons will take that option. It can be a win-win situation on both sides. The skills that many prisoners have can be used to help build societies on the African continent and also relieve the pressure on America. The money that is spent on the criminal justice system, the pain in the Black and Hispanic communities today, the single mothers, the children who travel to prisons every weekend are all criminal activities in itself. We must bring a stop to this.

I feel that America committed one of the greatest crimes against humanity by bringing our ancestors into slavery and then robbing them of the knowledge of themselves, making them feel that they were less than human beings, which psychologically affects our community today. The lack of proper self-esteem that is prevalent among Black people in America is directly related to the slavery experience. This is a tragic reality in American history.

Reparations are necessary. America must repair the damage. One way is to open the prison doors and allow negotiations to begin for our prisoners to build a new reality on the African continent.

63

Africa, America's Solution To The Prison Population

During the month of June, the National Newspaper Publishers Association (NNPA) held its annual convention in Memphis, Tennessee. I was honored by its president, Ms. Dorothy Leavell, to make a presentation on Africa. The title was, "Covering Africa." The conference was very successful and Ms. Leavell, as always, was a gracious hostess.

I have always had a great love for the Black press of America. At times, I feel they are not appreciated within our community or read by enough of us. I made a statement in my presentation that every Black household should read the Black press weekly and make sure they take out subscriptions. The Black press should be the heart and soul of the Black community, and must be respected.

At the end of the conference, I was invited to address the local mosque of the Nation of Islam. Minister Anthony Muhammad of Muhammad Mosque No. 55 had, over the past four years, extended numerous invitations for me to give a presentation. Finally, I was able to honor his request.

At the end of my lecture, I opened the floor for questions. A woman stood to ask a question about her son who was serving time in prison. While incarcerated, he accepted Islam under the leadership of Minister Louis Farrakhan. Her passionate plea for the brothers behind the prison walls of America was moving. It touched me deeply because this has been my passion for many, many years: How to help our brothers and sisters who are incarcerated.

I have lectured in prisons and listened to their side. I have watched the prison population escalate to more than 1.6 million inmates, at a growth of eight percent a year. Sometimes, it is difficult to distinguish fact from fiction about what is going on in America's prisons and penal system. Is it true that America has the largest prison population in the world? I know for sure that the prison population of America is larger than the population of 12 countries on the African continent. And many of these young men and women, depending on what state they are in, have faced judges who, in many cases, are giving out excessive amounts of time.

It is painful to read the letters of inmates or visit them and see this tremendous waste of human lives. I recently read a letter from an inmate with whom I had lost contact because he was transferred to another prison suddenly as part of the new private prison program. Prior to this transfer, he was in a prison just minutes away from his home, family and loved ones. However, because of the private prison nightmare creeping and growing in America, he was shipped from Smyrna (near Wilmington) in Delaware to Florence, Arizona.

How often can his family members, who are poor and struggling, make a trip to Arizona to visit him? Besides the torture of being incarcerated, the pain is doubled in being denied visitation from his family because of the hardship imposed on them to travel such a long distance.

AFRICA AND THE WORLD: REVISITED

I watched this in New York during the days that I would visit Danamora Prison, located in the farthest corner of the State of New York near the Canadian border. It was an 8-10 hour drive to reach the facility. America needs to look at her prison population because some say that it is 65 percent Black American. Others say it is 85 percent Blacks, Hispanics and Native Americans. Whatever the figure is, we know for sure that African Americans constitute the largest number of prisoners. There are now more than 200,000 women in prisons across America.

The Honorable Elijah Muhammad wrote 37 years ago in The Muslim Program that he wanted freedom for all the believers of Islam held in federal prisons as well as freedom for Black men and women now under the death sentence in prisons across America. On the same point, he said that we, Black people, should have the freedom to accept or reject being separated and establish a land of our own.

Minister Louis Farrakhan, in his book, "Torchlight For America," asked the question, "Why can't we work out a way, a deal, a compromise, a negotiation with the government of America and some governments on the African continent for those men and women who are doing between 5-40 years and even serving a life sentence in prison to be released to Africa, where they can begin to build a new reality for themselves as well as help African countries at the same time?"

There are many places in Africa where populations have been decimated or land is uncultivated because the climate is arid and there is no water. It may sound far-fetched and some people may say it has no logic or basis; the idea is crazy.

I am sure that when Europeans began to settle America and someone in England said, "We need people to go to this frontier land," many were not willing to go; but others went. This is how much of America was started. So, why don't we go to the prison houses to see if we can find those who would like to go to Africa? This is the same way Australia and New Zealand were established.

AKBAR MUHAMMAD

I hope that the African nations who possess tremendous amounts of land and have small populations would consider this as a solution. I look at the needs of African nations and I consider the fact that many of the men and women in the prisons of America are brilliant. Some of the best minds among Black people in America are being warehoused in the prisons of America. They need an opportunity. Whether it is the many who have made mistakes or the many who are innocent, they need an opportunity to build a new reality, a better life. As the discussion begins about the population of Africa being wiped out from AIDS, we have an opportunity to re-populate many countries of Africa.

In 1961, the Honorable Elijah Muhammad made an appeal in The Muslim Program for the United States government to free all of the inmates on death row. He didn't ask for freedom for the prisoners because he wanted to see criminals roaming the streets. He knew that these men and women were not their true selves. He felt that, if he had an opportunity to go into the prisons to teach them the knowledge of themselves, they would no longer desire to be criminals. They would come out of criminal thinking and behavior to become model citizens. His work continues today under the leadership of Minister Louis Farrakhan.

In 1998, from July 25 to August 2, the country of Ghana celebrated the first Emancipation Celebration held on the continent of Africa. During this week-long event, there were extensive discussions about the horrors of slavery.

In the last three years, we heard about one of the most vicious crimes since slavery. The American government and one of its agencies (the CIA) participated in the movement of drugs from Central America to America, in order to support the Contras (Counter Revolutionary Force) who were trying to overthrow the legitimate government of the Sandinistas in Nicaragua.

AFRICA AND THE WORLD: REVISITED

When Congress blocked the funding of the Contras, supporters of the Contras went to the Saudis, according to the book, "Veil" by Bob Woodward. They extracted $32 million from them. We do not know the full truth of it, but we have heard that the money, instead of being used to pay salaries and purchase more weapons, was invested in the movement of drugs into America that started this terrible drug epidemic of crack cocaine – a drug so potent that it can make you an addict after one try.

This same drug has brought total havoc to the Black community and has contributed to the swelling the American prison population. Crack cocaine has proliferated the gang battles in the streets of this country and has taken the lives of countless members of our community.

Now, the criminal judicial systems are jammed with young men and women plea-bargaining for their lives. Young men and women are going to prison, spending so many years behind bars. The prison has become a pressure cooker in America. The waste of lives is costing American taxpayers a tremendous amount of money. In some institutions, it costs America as much as $42,000 a year to house one inmate. The minimum cost now is about $20,000-$22,000 per year.

However, the state and federal government continue to spend this kind of money and continue to build more prisons every day. And now the private prison corporations are back in the picture, with prisons on the stock market. In spite of all the spending, there is no evidence of rehabilitation or reformation of these inmates. We need to look for an alternative.

AKBAR MUHAMMAD

This is an uphill struggle and I draw strength from men like W.E.B. Du Bois, who became active in this struggle at the turn of this century until 1963 at the age of 93 when he passed away. He said, "The question of the 21st century will be the question of color." He struggled for his people and he fought for his ideas. We must fight for the idea that these Black prisoners be given a new lease on life. If we were in any other country in the world, they would be considered political prisoners because of the racist politics of America. America based its economy on the idea of slavery and made it a legal institution.

I cannot emphasize enough the destruction and havoc that slavery caused in the Black community, even 135 years after the government declared it was abolished. The victims of this cruel system are still suffering.

Our brothers and sisters can become true assets to the nations of Africa, instead of liabilities of America. All of the skills and knowledge Black people have gained running and managing White America can be used on the African continent. We can be a great help to our brothers and sisters on the continent, but we need their interaction.

Many African governments and leaders will say this idea is insanity. They fear that the criminal problem will be transplanted from America to Africa. My answer is that these were the same brothers and sisters whose ancestors were kidnapped from Africa. In response to the cry for reparations for slavery, Europeans and Americans are researching and recording the involvement of African chiefs in the slave trade. Black Americans are echoing the same sentiments. This is a clear example of the old game of blaming the victim. Africa was victimized by Africa and Europe. Now, America and Europe are blaming Africans for the problem of slavery. How many times have we seen this ploy in history?

AFRICA AND THE WORLD: REVISITED

I firmly believe that slavery has twisted and mangled the thinking of Black men and women in America. Yes, many may be guilty of criminal acts. In legal circles and other circles, it is said that these Black criminals are "out of their minds." These men and women were not in their right minds because they were denied their right minds. They were robbed of their sound states of mind brought through the horrors of slavery. Currently in America, chattel slavery may not exist; however, the aftermath of the institution of slavery is glaringly present.

To this day, the American government has refused to apologize for slavery and refused to pay compensation in reparations for the years that we have suffered under whips and lashes. This treatment produced people who are not in their right minds. In America, there are numerous court cases where lawyers argued that their clients were "legally insane" at the time of the crimes and were not responsible for their actions.

Millions of Black Americans have been driven insane because of racism in America, oppression and the unequal treatment of a person due to the color of their skin. In addition to this, they have to struggle daily to maintain themselves in an unjust society. Many could not stand the pressure. They have lost their ability to cope with the basics of life.

Frederick Douglass, one of the Founding Fathers of Black thought, was very clear on the issues of slavery and liberation. He lamented over how we are still put upon to prove that we are men and women after all we have given to America and accomplished for America. His speech is timeless and it makes me reflect on the new slavery today – the American penal institution.

AKBAR MUHAMMAD

Douglass eloquently said:

"Would you have to argue that man is entitled to liberty? That he is the rightful owner of his own body. You have already declared it. Must I argue the wrongfulness of slavery? Is that a question for Republicans? Is it to be settled by the rules of logic and argumentation, as a matter beset with great difficulty, involving a doubtful application of the principle of justice hard to understand? How should I look today in the presence of Americans, dividing and subdividing a discourse, to show that men have a natural right to freedom, speaking of it relatively and positively, negatively and affirmatively."

XI
SOCIAL & CULTURAL CONNECTIONS: ESSENTIAL SOLUTIONS FOR CHANGE

AKBAR MUHAMMAD

Akbar Muhammad, Bobbi Humprey, Jerry Rawlings, James Mtume

64

Defining Cultural Independence

There are many definitions of culture. When you look at the meanings that are most common and list them, you cannot find any definitions independent of our experiences and relationships with Western thinking. These are some of the words that dictionaries use as synonymous with culture: cultivation, heritage, background, tradition, breeding, enlightenment, history, manners and mores.

When talking of cultural independence, you first have to talk about your cultural roots. Cultural roots for Black Americans began before slavery. Whatever was produced during slavery, we consider today our culture; however, that culture has a root. The actions of people in a nation always play a role in the advancement or decline of a culture.

During some of my lectures in the United States and abroad, I often quote the Honorable Minister Louis Farrakhan, leader of the Nation of Islam, who has the awesome ability while speaking to adjust his lecture to fit any type of audience.

"A study of history is to know what was, in order to understand what is, and make a projection on what is to be," says Minister Farrakhan when responding to those who may feel that the history of slavery, especially its brutality, should never be publicly addressed.

AKBAR MUHAMMAD

As I repeat Minister Farrakhan's words, I am reminded of an African symbol – a cultural sign that shows our foreparents shared the same insights. The African symbol called "Sankofa" is that of a bird with his body and feet facing in one direction and his head leaning over his shoulder, looking back in the opposite direction. Minister Farrakhan states that, in order to go forward, you must know from whence you came.

Whatever remains of our culture that have survived slavery has been synthesized with our slave and post-slavery experiences. Our way of speaking, music, worship service and literature have all been influenced by our experiences. From our beginnings in Africa, throughout our slavery sojourn, up to our present circumstances, all have played a part in who and what we are.

I was recently in Libya at the Extraordinary 4th Meeting of the Organization of African Unity (OAU). It was a very historic gathering, pulling together 43 African heads of state. According to various news reports, this particular OAU summit was the largest gathering of African heads of state since the OAU celebrated its 30-year anniversary in Cairo, Egypt in 1993. The purpose of the 4th OAU meeting was to take a serious look at making a United States of Africa.

During this historic summit, Libyan television played the miniseries "Roots," which was watched by many summit delegates. The following morning, the conversation among the delegates was "Roots." The delegates who watched were getting an insight into some of the cultural nuances of Africans in the Diaspora who have experienced the horrors of slavery. The most striking comment came from one of the Nation of Islam delegates, Mustapha Farrakhan.

"I thought I was over this [slavery]," he said. His voice breaking, he continued, "Last night, I cried as I watched 'Roots' again." After the room became silent, the son of Minister Farrakhan gathered his thoughts and said that, when he returns to the States, he plans to have all five of his children sit down and watch every episode of "Roots." These responses took place two generations after the events depicted and 23 years since "Roots" first aired on national television. Our slave history has definitely had an impact on our culture.

We can never have cultural independence until we understand what our forefathers suffered during this horrible experience. In order to understand cultural independence, we must find a way to deal with our identity crisis, the problem of self-esteem, and obtaining an in-depth knowledge of self.

We must have a knowledge of our ancestors and traditions – a knowledge of our history so that we can be educated and enlightened. We must be able to understand what happened during the breeding process that took place on slave plantations. We must understand what racism in this society produced in us in the form of manners and mores.

AKBAR MUHAMMAD

65

Africa and Asia Take a First Step in Fighting Western Cultural Imperialism

The African country of the Gambia and the country of Indonesia in the southeast of Asia, which has the largest Muslim population in the world, have delivered the first blow against the rising tide of cultural imperialism emanating from the West.

The Head of State of the Gambia and Chairman of the Armed Forces Provisional Ruling Council, Captain Yahya A.J.J. Jammeh (as of January 1, 1996) implemented a decree that outlaws the sale, use or possession of bleaching cream, also known as lightening or whitening cream in Africa. The Gambian decree number 65, cited as the Skin Bleaching (Prohibition) Decree, which has observed the long-term physical and psychological effects of using these products, deserves acknowledgment from the medical profession. If the spirit of this law can move across the continent of Africa, it will do a great service to women who are victimized by the cultural imperialism that promotes the idea that lightened skin is better than the Black beautiful skin with which God has blessed them.

AKBAR MUHAMMAD

President Mohammad Suharto of Indonesia recently banned Indonesian women from participating in beauty contests abroad. He made the decree after the recent Miss Universe Pageant in Las Vegas, Nevada. According to a statement from Suharto's Minister of Women's Affairs, Ms. Mien Sugandhi, the decree was a result of the public outcry over the participation of Alya Rohali, who was crowned Miss Indonesia in 1996. She appeared in Las Vegas in a one-piece swimsuit. With a population approaching 195 million people, of which 88-90 percent are Muslim, Indonesians viewed her appearance as shameful to Indonesian women, according to Ms. Sugandhi. She stressed that, in reference to Western-style beauty pageants, "They are not invited and will not be received."

These are major steps against cultural imperialism.

66

A Family Reunion

Imam Warith Deen Mohammed and Minister Louis Farrakhan

At the close of the first Black History Month of this new century, our community witnessed a family reunion that will be written in the pages of history – an Islamic Family Reunion. The vision held by Minister Louis Farrakhan and many others was fulfilled in Chicago as two great men announced their commitment to work together for the cause of Islam, prayed together and shared the platform.

AKBAR MUHAMMAD

As the International Representative of the Nation of Islam and Assistant to Minister Farrakhan, I know of the desire of both sides to work together for the betterment of our people. In August 1983, Imam Warithu Deen Muhammad and Minister Farrakhan met to talk about working in unity. I believe that the hearts of both men were hungry for unity, for the good of Islam and the salvation of many African Americans who are troubled and cannot seem to find their way to a better quality of life in America. For 17 years, words got in the way of what both hearts wanted.

The year that Minister Farrakhan spent out of public life, wrestling with the side effects of treatments he had in his battle against prostate cancer, he reflected on his vision of unity. He has said to me on many occasions, "Should Allah take our lives today, what legacy will we leave for our children and grandchildren? What will history say of us during the time when we were at the helm of our ships? We must make the steps in words and actions that we can forge this unity."

My heart was overjoyed to see these two men smiling at each other, praying together and pledging to work together. This is what we all wanted to see and hear. The press is suggesting that Minister Farrakhan is moving away from his nationalistic position. This is its attempt to send signals to struggling Black communities around the world that Minister Farrakhan will not be the strong voice for the issues and concerns that affect us. As Minister Farrakhan said in his keynote address, "I have not and will not abandon my Black brothers and sisters."

I have known him since 1961 and have worked with him since 1965. I can tell you with certainty that Minister Farrakhan loves Allah (God), his faith and Black people. He is a defender of our causes and is committed to Black people who are struggling under the yoke of injustice.

Everything must change. That is the nature of life. Has Farrakhan changed? I can say Minister Farrakhan has changed. I feel that Allah (God) has shown him the way to fulfill a vision he has had since 1977 when we started on the road to rebuild the Nation of Islam. He and thousands of other Muslims who grew into maturity in the Nation of Islam longed to be one! Longed to be together! Longed to use what had been handed down to Muslims under the guidance of the Honorable Elijah Muhammad to better the condition of our people.

Yes, Minister Farrakhan has changed. He has moved to a new level. Let us who know the importance of unity give this new marriage of two Islamic communities time to work out the "kinks." It may be difficult at times, but it is a marriage of necessity. Long live the unity of these two communities. Long live the vision of Imam Muhammad and Minister Farrakhan!

AKBAR MUHAMMAD

AFRICA AND THE WORLD: REVISITED

67

SOLVING THE PROBLEM OF LANGUAGE:

A FAILURE TO COMMUNICATE

Language is used as a form of communication. As we have seen by the recent discussions in Oakland, California, there is still a failure to communicate between White and Black people.

If they had not robbed us of our language when we arrived in America as their slaves, then maybe we could at least communicate with one another. If the arriving Europeans to Africa had taken time to study our indigenous African languages, they would have had more respect for us and our ability to convey thoughts. Perhaps, the ones who need to learn this so-called "Black English" or "Ebonics" are the ones who teach.

There are many countries that have what is called a colloquial language or slang; however, the education texts are always in the classic or original language. It seems the problem here is arrogance.

Since America is considered the world's melting pot, it seems that it should be able to incorporate some diversity by learning pre-existing languages, not so-called Black English.

I have been blessed to travel to 95 countries in the world in service for the Nation of Islam. Out of the 95 countries, I have been to 31 African countries. I have learned to love and respect the languages of my brothers and sisters on the continent. I have heard stories from the Africans of how the Europeans, White Americans and even a few Black Americans who are always busy trying to act like their "masters" have no respect for local languages, and have no desire to learn them even after living in Africa for years.

AKBAR MUHAMMAD

It never ceases to amaze me how an African brother or sister with no "formal education" or training can handle four or five languages. There is a joke in Africa that I often repeat to my guests on the continent. When you find a person who speaks three languages, what do you call him or her? Trilingual.

When you find a person who speaks two languages, what do you call him or her? Bilingual. When you find a person who only speaks one language and is proud of it, what do you call him or her? American.

AFRICA AND THE WORLD: REVISITED

A. Akbar Muhammad

ABOUT THE AUTHOR

Akbar Muhammad is a Historian and Consultant on International Affairs, Africa and the Middle East. He has traveled to and met top diplomatic officials to over 154 countries around the world—including 44 African nations—and has lived in Ghana, Africa for over a decade.

Through the Africa and Middle East Literacy Foundation, he continues to consult with African and world leaders to promote humanitarian efforts in many parts of the world, including galvanizing business and political leaders from the Diaspora to work in Africa and other developing nations.

In 2007, he organized a historic trip for a press delegation to travel to the Sudan for a visit to Darfur on a fact-finding mission, and through his efforts secured exclusive one-on-one interviews with Sudan's President Omar El-Bashir for Black Entertainment Television (BET) and the TV-One Network.

He dedicates his time speaking and encouraging others to travel, work and do business in Africa. Over the years, he has accompanied and arranged travel to Africa for thousands of experienced and first-time travelers including notable celebrities, major sports figures and influential civic and business leaders. His extensive work and travel in Africa are reflected in his column "Africa and the World" which is published in African American newspapers nationally.

He is a recipient of an Honorary Doctorate Degree from the Global Evangelical Christian Seminary at the University of Alabama. He is the founder of Youth4Africa Foundation, a non-profit organization based on the belief that young Blacks in the Diaspora are due a personal journey "Back to Africa" to gain a historical perspective that reconnects lost cultural traditions of the past to present life choices. He believes "Taking Young People to Africa Can Make a Difference." The Africa experience will aid our youth to understand their purpose, inspire fundamental discussions and shape positive self-images.

AKBAR MUHAMMAD

AFRICA AND THE WORLD: REVISITED
INDEX

Abdoulaye Wade   64

Abdul Salam Abubakar   50, 51, 236

Ahmad Tejan Kabbah   29

Ahmed Ben Bella   44

Al Sharpton   176-77

Algeria   44, 104, 111

Alice Windom   47

Amiri Baraka (Leroi Jones)   222

Andrew Young   108, 141-42

Ange-Felix Patasse   91, 99

Angola   64, 101, 111, 112, 131, 136, 149, 150, 190, 191, 227

Bakili Muluzi   90, 93

Benin   3, 91, 93, 104, 175

Blaise Compaore   90, 173

Botswana   93, 109, 125, 156

Burkina Faso   21, 23, 90, 173

Burundi   3

Cameroon   93

Central African Republic   21, 93, 99, 149

Chad   21, 90, 91, 99, 149, 150

Charles Taylor   26, 90, 99, 161, 162-68, 171-74

Che Guevara   214-15

Comoros   4, 91

Coretta Scott King   109

Cote d'Ivoire   29, 108, 109, 172, 202, 230

Cuba   214, 227, 235

Daniel Ortega   63

Democratic Republic of Congo (formerly Zaire)   21, 63, 64, 71, 72, 73, 90, 93, 107, 111, 112, 121, 161, 162, 213-15, 227

Dexter Gordon   47

Diana Ross   81-82

Dick Gregory   109

Djibouti   21

Dorothy Height   109

Earl Shinhoster   77-79

Edward Wilmot Blyden   143

Egypt   27, 32, 71, 91, 99, 100, 136, 142, 254

Elijah Muhammad   68, 69, 84, 117, 193-97, 200, 220, 221, 245, 246, 261

Eritrea   15, 21, 107, 111, 129, 131, 136, 165, 166, 177

Ethiopia   15, 49, 107, 111, 129, 131, 136, 165, 166, 177

Fidel Castro   227, 235

Frederick Chiluba   28, 33, 36

Frederick Douglass   249

Gabon   93, 149, 150

Gamal Abdel Nasser   32

Gambia   3, 21, 49, 59, 60, 90, 257

George Padmore   47

Ghana   3, 4, 6, 29, 32, 41, 45-48, 53, 54, 87, 100, 108-112, 121, 129, 141, 142, 172, 173, 199, 201-203, 208, 227, 246

Guinea   32, 111, 149, 150

Hosni Mubarak   100

Hugh Sheare   69

Hugo Chavez   150

Idriss Debby   90

Indonesia   257, 258

Jamaica   68, 69, 227

James Baldwin   47

Jamil Al-Amin   118

Jeremiah Wright   132

Jerry John Rawlings   54, 108, 109, 141, 142, 201-03

Jesse Jackson   49, 67, 69, 108, 189, 192, 235

Jewel Howard Taylor   51, 77, 144, 147

Joaquim Chissano   29

John Garang   15, 16, 112, 128, 131, 132, 135, 136, 168, 177

John Kufuor   172

Jonas Savimbi   101, 111, 131, 149, 190

Jose Eduardo dos Santos   64

Joseph Mobutu   71-73, 117, 162, 214, 215, 227

Jules Wijdendasch   109

Julius Nyerere   44

Kenneth Kaunda   44

Kenya   15, 22, 109, 125, 129, 131, 135, 136, 156, 176, 177

Kwame Nkrumah   32, 41, 44, 47, 49, 109, 121, 199, 227

Kwame Ture   4, 44

Laurent Kabila   64, 71, 90, 213-215

Leon Sullivan   50, 107, 112

Leonard Jeffries   108

Liberia   25, 26, 51, 77, 78, 90, 93, 97, 99, 100, 107, 124, 143-147, 167,168, 169, 171-174, 212, 227

Libya   11, 12, 15, 18-23, 25, 27, 32, 34, 36, 43, 44, 61-63, 71, 75, 76, 89-91, 97-99, 136-38, 149, 150, 162, 168, 173, 192, 227, 254

Louis Farrakhan   17, 20, 27, 28, 31-33, 36, 39, 40, 43, 56-65, 67-69, 71, 75, 108, 124, 128, 130, 132, 138, 156, 176, 190, 192, 194, 202, 220, 235, 240, 244-46, 253, 254, 259-61

Malawi   21, 90, 93, 207

Malcolm X   36, 57, 59, 68, 109

Mali   21, 64, 90

Marcus Garvey   109, 144, 199, 200

Martin Luther King Jr.   109, 226

Mauritania   127, 137, 138

Maya Angelou   47

Michael Manley   69, 227

Mozambique   29, 58, 112, 131, 136, 186

Muammar Qadhafi   11-20, 21-24, 25, 27, 28, 32, 34, 35-37, 43, 44, 61-65, 76, 89-91, 99, 138, 156, 162, 173, 215, 227

Muhammad Ali   69, 73, 83, 84, 115-18

Mumia Abu Jamal (H. Rap Brown)   118

Namibia   21, 29, 64, 73, 93, 125, 156, 230

Nelson Mandela   18, 90, 185, 187

Nicaragua   63, 246

Niger   21, 91

Nigeria   4, 6, 29, 50, 89, 91, 94, 109, 150, 173, 211, 212, 236

Olusegun Obasanjo   29, 173

Omar al-Bashir   29, 99, 109, 128

Omar Bongo   150

Oumar Konare   64, 90

Patrice Lumumba   44, 72, 162, 214, 227

Paul Kigame   64

Richard Wright   47

Robert Mugabe   29, 64, 97, 109, 123, 155, 168, 171, 205-09

Robert Taylor   146

Rwanda   3, 64, 161, 162, 213, 215

Sam Njoma   64

Samuel Doe   173

Sani Abacha   211

Saudi Arabia   18, 75, 100, 150

Sekou Ture   32

Senegal   53, 60, 64, 109

Siad Barre   202

Sierra Leone   29, 97, 99, 107, 109, 111, 171, 172, 173, 190, 212

Somalia   29, 93, 94, 97, 98, 107, 112, 202

South Africa   28, 29, 58, 64, 73, 91, 101-03, 120-22, 125, 156, 168, 173, 178, 185, 186, 190, 191, 206, 219, 222, 223, 229

Sudan   15, 16, 21, 29, 89, 97-99, 107, 109, 112, 127-29, 131, 132, 135-38, 149, 150, 165, 168, 175-78

Suriname   109

Susan Taylor   109

Swaziland   109

Tanzania   44, 109, 135, 208

Thabo Mbeki   29, 103, 173

Togo   93, 109

Tunisia   90

Uganda   15, 29, 58, 64, 90, 93, 107, 112, 128, 129, 131, 133, 136, 161, 176-78,

213, 215, 230

Venezuela   150

Warithu Deen Muhammad   260

W.E.B. Du Bois   39-41, 47, 248

Yahya Jaameh   90, 257

Yemen   97, 98

Yoweri Museveni   29, 64, 90, 112, 230

Zaire *see Democratic Republic of Congo*

Zambia   27, 28, 31, 33, 35, 44, 102, 125, 156, 207

Zimbabwe   29, 64, 97, 109, 123-25, 155, 156, 168, 169, 171, 174, 206-09

Zine el-Abidine Ben Ali   90

ARTICLE CATALOGUE

1. My Love of Africa   1
2. Airport Blues for the African in Europe   4
3. Colonel Muammar Qadhafi Speaks on Reparations to Black Americans for Slavery and a United States of Africa   10
4. Re-examining Muammar Gadhafi's Call for a United States of Africa   26
5. Will The African Union Be Delayed by September 11?   32
6. United States of Africa – The End of the Organization of African Unity and the Birth of the African Union   35
7. Farrakhan Calls for Support for African Union   39
8. W.E.B. DuBois Submitting to the Call of Africa   51
9. Qadhafi's Call for Reparations and A Historic Meeting of African Leaders in Libya   55
10. Africa in the Diaspora and Africans at Home, We Need Each Other   58
11. Building Bridges, Building Hope and The African Agenda 2000   65
12. Through the Door of No Return   69
13. The National Agenda and Africa   74
14. Alex Haley Mosque and School to Open in The Gambia   77
15. Let Farrakhan Have The Money   80
16. Farrakhan's Africa Trip: Prelude to Million Family March   83
17. Louis Farrakhan at 70: His Impact   87
18. The Death of Mobuto   93
19. A Special Ramadan for the People of Libya   98
20. The Untimely Death of Earl T. Shinhoster…His Struggle Must Continue   101
21. Diana Ross, Wake Up and Smell the Coffee   105
22. My Ali Story   108

23. Can Western-Style Democracy Benefit Africa?   113

24. Libya, France and America: The African Agenda   116

25. The Impact of America's Tragedy on the Nations of Africa   120

26. America's War! Is Africa The Next Target?   125

27. The Palestinian Struggle: Africa Can Make A Difference   131

28. Media Coverage and The Fifth African/African American Summit Conference   138

29. African Bloodletting, The Betrayal of Africans in The Diaspora   144

30. Ali, Just Say No!   149

31. Israel's Dirty Work in Africa   156

32. Zimbabwe: Taking Back Land from White May Be Contagious   162

33. Show "Touched By An Angel" to Highlight Sudanese Slave Controversy   167

34. The Sudan and Slavery Issue   173

35. America's Failed Policy in The Sudan   178

36. One More Big Lie: America Accuses Libya of Slavery   182

37. Planning For The Future? Consider Africa   187

38. Liberia Can Be Rebuilt   190

39. Black Farmers For Africa   193

40. Bush Dismisses Black America, As He Targets West African Oil   197

41. Stolen Land, White Occupation   202

42. Africa and The Effects of Euro-Tourism   206

43. American President's Hypocrisy Toward Africa   210

44. War in Africa: The Root of Conflict Between Eritrea and Ethiopia   214

45. President Charles Taylor and The Liberian People   217

46. Why Liberia? Why President Charles Taylor?   46

47. The Question of Slavery in Africa   227

48. Why A Strike on Iraq Just Before Religious Holidays?   234

49. Nelson Mandela on President Bush: "No Foresight – He Can't Think Properly" 238

50. Target Jesse Jackson: The Dismantling of A Black Leader 243

51. New Book on The Honorable Elijah Muhammad: Truth Mixed With Falsehood and Outright Lies 250

52. Remembering Marcus Garvey 258

53. Ghana in Transition, When The Strong Man Goes 261

54. Stand Up For President Robert Mugabe 266

55. The Death of General Sani Abacha 273

56. The Death of Lauren Kabila: The Man Who Wouldn't Be America's Boy 276

57. Reparations Take Center Stage 282

58. Apologies Are In Order 290

59. Why Is It So Difficult for President Clinton to Apologize for Slavery? 296

60. Correcting A Historical Wrong: The Struggle for Quotas 301

61. An Appeal to Reverend Jesse Jackson: Work To Liberate The Other Captives 304

62. Can Africa Help America Solve Its Prison Crisis? 308

63. Africa, America's Solution to the Prison Population 314

64. Defining Cultural Independence 327

65. Africa and Asia Take A First Step In Fighting Western Cultural Imperialism 331

66. A Family Reunion 333

67. Solving The Problem of Language: A Failure to Communicate 337

$$\begin{array}{r} 12\overset{9}{0}03 \\ -21 \\ \hline 823 \end{array} \qquad \begin{array}{r} 1203 \\ 21 \end{array}\Big)\begin{array}{l} 82 \\ 03 \\ \hline 85 \end{array}$$